To Brother Mack
Judy & Barbara

Thanks for the support and
inspiration. Last year is when we're
better together, and this year we're
of being Married and doing it.

Wedding fest / Marriage retreat
2017
4/14/17

Poetically Inclined

Raw and Uncut

Ervin Miller Jr.

authorHOUSE®

AuthorHouse™
1663 Liberty Drive
Bloomington, IN 47403
www.authorhouse.com
Phone: 1 (800) 839-8640

Published by AuthorHouse 01/22/2016

ISBN: 978-1-5049-7152-2 (sc)
ISBN: 978-1-5049-7131-7 (e)

Library of Congress Control Number: 2015921472

Print information available on the last page.

Dedication

First and foremost, I must undoubtedly give props to my source and my strength; the greatest power in my life and this universe- my lord and Savior Jesus Christ. For without "You" this project would've stayed doomed from its birth year in 2008. So I would like to give my appreciation through my thanks. In 2010, I never thought I would ever be able to say this, but thank you to the four guys that stole my 2005 Chevy Malibu; and my first manuscript that was on a flash-drive within it. For without your actions these reactions would've never existed. I thank you because we are forever linked now, as you helped created this too. I pray each and every one of you brothas success, and the second chance everyone should be entitled to; so make the best of it. Next, I would like to dedicate this to those of you who really helped me and motivated me during this depression period. This includes my family, friends, and loved ones.

I also want to thank those of you that allowed me to write a reflection of your mental vision, that you knew not how to story tell. This also goes forth to those that hope, dream, and inspire to be great. I want to give a shout out to those that understand their gifts/talents and callings. I've also seen and met people in this world that still yearn to make a difference in this world. I'm deeply touched by these individuals that want to be prominent figures. When I closed my eyes, it was at that moment that I saw visions of young leaders that dared to be diverse, and with a true thirst. These people are those that are defiant when they need to be, and the ones that rewrote an old book of generational curses. This is for those that insist that different must exist. I say thank you to all of you. For it's because of you all that life will never be just black and white. You're the true visionaries, the trendsetters, party starters, and overall; great upcoming future leaders of tomorrow. Be different and stay comforted by your unique individuality that acts as a zebra stripes, or male peacock's feathers. Understand that you aren't wrong for wanting to set fire to the box, for you are unorthodox!

However, respect the differences you see, especially in those that live in the box. For just like you, we need them too.

I want to give a sincere thank you, to the students that attend SCAD, AWOL, and the momentary disabled gentlemen I've had the honor encountering and connecting with in the Habersham YMCA, in Savannah, Ga. Ladies and gentlemen I say thank you to each of you, for you all have truly inspired, and motivated through your abundant gifts, fight, grit and resolve, that are consistently put on display. You give to the members of the YMCA, the community, the city of Savannah, and because of this, I would like to give thanks to you all.

Last, but certainly not least, I would like to give very special thanks to my wife for putting up with my passion which is my other love, and my beautiful and handsome children. Remember, I draw strength from you guys; and seeing the smiles on each of your face, keeps me in the depths of this place.

Now if you don't know as of this moment, what your gifts and or talents- just remember it all starts with; what you can do the best at, with the least amount of effort. But understand, that life is made that much easier when you know your calling and understand your purpose. Thus, everything else will ultimately fall in line with these things, including school. Allow no room for wasted motion or time. For time is valuable and of the essence; so make your next move your latest best move.

Contents

Raw an uncut
Pt. 2

Forward

This book of poems was created to reach two sets of people: One being the spiritual people, and the other being the world. This started as a diary of sorts, as I captured the battle that wages daily between my flesh and spirit man. But along the way, this diary transformed into something more. This process became the silent cries of the mute, the whisper of the wind, the issues of the streets, and the everyday components that make this journey enjoyable, daunting, intimidating, exhilarating, breathtaking, sad, and pulse altering. Without the Lord's guidance I would've gave up, after I made it to sixty five poems; only to have them deleted. I've known that there must have been something special about this project, as the enemy still felt the need to attack it; after "You" spoke through my pastor Kenneth Rouche' to give me the encouragement and prayer to move forward. Then came the incident that occurred with my book saved on a flashdrive. The flash drive was never recovered, after being left in my car that was stolen.

However, this journey has truly taught me that writing is still a source of freedom for me. It's the ultimate get away; like vacationing spot. It's here, that I've been able to release my true creative nature and limitless unlocked potential. Within writing, I find a bond and a suited outlet. This is my tool that helps me give back through my point of view. Moreover, this is the understanding, in which I accept my divine God given calling. This project is the testament of the resolve that God placed within me, along with that never quit mentality and drive. The pieces featured in this book are primarily from the frame of 08-10. It was within this time frame that my life and view would change on primary issues such as my spirit vs my flesh. This stage set the tone for this book only being two chapters, which shows a silent struggle taking shape. My biggest inspiration came directly from the mirror, as it showcased what could never be hidden. It was there that I was able to see into the gateway of my own soul. It showed my flaws, my success, my many masks, and the internal lies we try to tell ourselves. I felt my own monumental strides, and saw my rock bottom decline. At my lowest point, I finally understood the battle, and how it wasn't one of flesh and blood; however, that it was true spiritual warfare. I learned to respect the truth, and see this world through another set of eyes; and from two viewpoints when needed. This journey truly became more than a project; it became a diary of sorts, as well as my main resort. It also became an awaken voyage, that saw me survive turbulent uncharted territory; and bring back with me the proof; that I'm "Poetically Inclined" and "Raw and Uncut".

This book's artwork was the result of a quartet type of collaboration by Michael Hines, Alexis Perez, Kyndall R. Bennett, and David Mahone.

Poetically Inclined

Pt.1

Poetically Inclined

Back with a different topic; real face, no costume.
So many unasked questions that I could answer, so why assume?
The flow is brain food, so thoughts are consumed.
I'm resting in this enclosure, like a baby in the womb stretching
for more room.
I try to make conversation make sense.
After all, I was, I am, and I will forever be far from dense.
I state this past, present, and future tense.
This book here is my house, and I'm letting you enter from the fence.
I deliver news like Bryant Gumbel.
I try to stay supported and avoid a costly stumble.
But if I fall, I pick myself up, remaining loyal to the process and humble.
'Cause the enemy has boxing gloves on, so it's time to rumble.
I carry a mouthpiece to avoid the slightest negative mumble.
I love what God has me doing; this is more than getting paid.
But I take no credit—I know I'm God-made.
This is one job that doesn't layoff.
Even if I'm sick, it helps treat my cough.
I sail through uncertain seas with the best captain.
My language should be universal, so I could even speak Latin.
But it would differ when it reached the people in Manhattan.
I try to keep my wordage straight-laced,
However sometimes the truth is hard to embrace,
So for some, it's like drinking hard alcohol with no chase.
But still I do what I have to in order to speak to the public-
with a strong type of bass.
Something that's real … you can feel,
No matter your color or race.

The Entrance

It's like ready, set, go; the author is back with more
Still trying to hone his point; sharper than a thumb-tact
Come on in;
Whatever you do, just don't rob yourself by skipping straight to
the end,
'Cause this is only the beginning of the next edition—
Code named "the new mission"
Constantly repairing and fine-tuning like a technician
Back on the elevator we go; rising above the last level
But when you step foot off, beware of the two-sided hall
The interesting thing is that both sides will make you pick, causing
you to stall,
but you're not to pick either; just follow the spotlight
'Cause it's a detailed icon, showing you the way that's right,
For between action and reaction, good and bad, fact or fiction,
sanity or insanity, it's a fine line
So follow each word, which acts as the next step under the lights
as you continue to shine
But one important note: if you get lost, just rewind;
So without further delay, it's now that time

More or Less

I'm not the definition of an iconic hero
But on the contrary, I'm by no means a zero
Why would I sell myself for less
I'm so full of will power; I truly confess
The controversial hot topics and heated issues I lay to rest
So here lies my accomplishments and faults,
yep, in that locked vault
Peacefully resting six feet deep,
so there's no need to weep
Or listen for the outcries,
'cause like the phoenix, situations still arise
Who am I? Well, understand that "I'm here 4 a reason"
I am the same guy, different look; entirely a new season
I'm back with a feeling like this is the third time
This time a little more defined, but still poetically inclined
Back with a little bit of an edge,
including a new outer hedge
This time no doors closed or shut
Making for an experience that's raw and uncut

Short and Sweet

You're beautiful;
from this day forward.
don't you get close to a mirror,
and wish you were dead,
'Cause you're beautiful—
regardless of what anybody says

My Brother's Keeper

We arrived from the same place,
I before you, but together we left stitches as a trace
We're nearly separated by five and a half years of space
You've longed to catch me, so you constantly give chase
But I haven't left you, and I never will; I'm in some of the features
of your face
No matter how much the enemy tries, this brotherly love can't be erased

I understand that some people want to give up on you
And understand this to be true, but those are judgmental views
See, those don't matter; its vanity, for there are those who believe
in you,
Even if you feel their numbers are a limited few
Take hold to God, and make a vow with him like I do
Keep your head on the swivel; watch out for those who call
themselves your ace,
You'd be surprised at those, waiting for the opportunity to take
your place
But never resort to revenge; forget them. They'll be judged
according to their own race
And lastly, never hold on to anger, letting it become hatred, because
that's a horrific case

There's Nothing New

Under the sun—you know the saying
There's nothing new,
Everything is updated,
Meaning it's already been done
So styles can't classify old or young
I'm talking about everything under this sun
That's why you need to know—what goes around
Most certainly will come back around,
And what goes up, you can most definitely believe,
It'll fall right back down
That's why you need to throw up a smile and
Disregard receiving a frown
So try passing around uplifting information
And watch how your mind stays sound
This even goes for that girl you thought was old game;
To the next, she could be that much-needed change
That he throws into his hall of fame
That's why a fool will throw away a dollar bill
In the form of change
And the wise will put it all up and make a decent exchange

Time Will Tell

Today I write you, uncertain in my mind,
But still unconditional from the heart is my love
I protect you like a lioness protects her cub
We grew together, but now we need time apart
The thought alone made me swallow hard
And taste sweet and bitter flavors like a tart
We're spacing out of each other's solar system
But I don't want to lose you like the others, whose
names I prefer not to list them
And when some have asked those business digging questions,
I give that shame-on-them look
And answer, "that part hasn't been written in our illustrious book"

Time Traveling

Letters make the smooth words that you speak
As seconds create the minutes that subliminally make your emotions weak
The hours mark the long-awaited day's transformation into weeks,
In which you're no longer meek
Now time has transcended into months of raw, accumulated emotion
By the dawn of the New Year, you're very much looking forward to that promotion
Yeah, that brushed-aside incident has become recurring like the rent
You think to question where the time went and the actions speak well spent,
For each letter spoke the vow
Unexplainably, seconds sprinted by, leaving your memory asking when, where, and how
Next you witness sixty steps transcend a minute's meaning of now
Unwillingly they fold to usher in new months and new years
Then you're rudely disturbed from the sounds of champagne glasses coming together before the cheers

Nightmare

Each time we write, my feelings grow stronger
Love is making this history, so the timeline just grows longer
Speaking fluent body language is how we communicate
Our hearts seem to relate
God forbid if life was to bring you any harm,
I would be struck by an unkind alarm

Like, life reacting as an immoral type of judge
Who sentenced you to life without memory of us two
What would I do,
if every day you looked at me, and saw nothing but an unclear clue?
What could I do,
if I felt like deep down the truth you knew?
But what would I do,
if you gave me a long, deep stare?
What could I do,
I guess stop sweating and just wake up from my nightmare…

Until We Meet Again

It's kind of funny how I reminisce on you,
Like the season is still the decisive fall of '02
Reality becomes overtaken by denial, making the truth untrue
Since your departure, the sky won't even stay blue,
So I pay tribute to you from my point of view

Until we meet again

It stays polar cold; without your love that warms better than any
heater or cover,
We're closer than knots in shoelaces and more heartfelt than the
relationship of two lovers
That's why our relationship will remain untouchable like no others.
This includes the one I share with my loving mother
It still can't interact with the bonded love that I had for another
She was the majestic queen, if ever the 'hood had a mighty castle
She was the heartbeat, if ever the 'hood had a pure and caring system
She was the lead instrument to an unprecedented symphony,
And when she left, the ears that heard that beautiful symphony
went deaf

Bye-Bye

I was frozen solid just twenty-four hours ago
Hurt is now present, along with my tarnished male ego
I may have watched someone so special up and leave
With quick beats from my heart, I had the chance, I do believe,
But when I had my opportunity to verbally exhale, I
Choked 'cause it became hard to breathe

You knew that I froze; maybe that's why you smiled
You delivered a wave, which resulted in my insides running wild
I wanted to speak up, but my bass wouldn't speak out, clear and loud
So I was left standing soaked under a raincloud
What happened to me? I picked the perfect day to seem mellow
and mild
Thank God there wasn't a crowd,
And to think I didn't even say hi or bye-bye.

The tourist

Trying to adjust to all that accompanies the Savannah River
His eyes make a brief landfall; on the downtown cobble stone
Allowing his eyes to become a part of Savannah's history
He's astounded, although his facial features read that of a mystery
The strange thing is; for the first time he recognizes that it too has
a task
He stands and watches; as thoughts become questions; he doesn't
think to ask
He begins wondering, how they maintain the upkeep, of this aged
cobblestoned street
But he doesn't lose track of this vibe, 'cause for the moment his
eyes play hide and seek
His eyes are locked in, but he manages to multitask with his
sensitive ears
Have you seen her, is what he quickly hears
He follows his sense, and sees her; replying to his wife yes dear
What he sees is a large stoned size female, with a historical tale
His mind must conceive her tarnished glory, so his eyes tell her
unique story
Standing in her own world; stood the famous waving girl

Lil Mz. Jiga Boo

Lil' Mz. Jiga Boo
The name is self explanatory
Rhythm to her ears is very mandatory
She is who she is
The ever moving kid; is a wiz
In the spotlight on the dance floor; she handles her biz
She makes her body language speak hours of rehearsal
Making her moves far spread; like they're universal
She causes mouths to drop; she's the act, which seems impossible
to top
Mz. Jiga Boo, seems to own, every old or new move
Simply doing what she does the best, which is groove
Sometimes raw & uncut; but yet polished and smooth
So untouchable on the dance floor –
her haters can't help but to adore
She's the image of geography;
created through her own choreography
Able to display the spirit of the weather through a rain dance
Any move shown to her; she can reenact or enhance
Never cocky but rather sure of herself, more like confident
Every move is what it needs to be; rather graceful or intense, it's
clearly evident

The pianist

At a pack house
The curtains rise, and suddenly you can't hear a mouse
He starts off with a hello
That's staged A-capella
He prepares to perform
Changing the forecast of this silent storm
He prepares to alter the present atmosphere
Atmosphere is his canvas;
making his hands the brush that he smears
And as he plays thousands are affected through the doorways of
their ears
He simply manipulates feelings through this rectangular object
For the moment musically interfering with mental logic
His fingers dance
And your emotions enhance
He then reaches the climatic point; which brings a momentary pause
Then precisely thereafter comes a thunderous applause
And you take a moment for the cause
He dresses the part; no incognito
This brother is clearly fashioned with the latest tuxedo
His fingers appear to be walking
Better yet talking
Everything coordinated; featuring black and white
Leaving only enough action sitting below the spotlight
The musical notes on qeue, with precise follow through
He gives a world renowned show
Like his setting was at the world famous Apollo
After all, everyone came in hopes of getting their money's worth
But never suspected they would witness pure musical fingers give
birth …
"The pianist"

Unstable environment

In this courtroom, I see a circus
The lawyer is the ventriloquist
And the judge appears to be the clown
with bad jokes
It seems like a huge hocus
The plaintiff gets provoked and the sentence is invoked

Speculation

He bought a new fully loaded car
The color was black, darker than tar
She heard him on the phone
Stating man, with a body like that, I couldn't wait to get her home
So she soon made it her business, not to give him any space alone
Each day she caught him on the phone
admitting how he adored her;
making the other jealous
His mind stayed all on her; like a hot dog covered in relish
She sat back with steam rising from her scalp
And he spent his every moment talking about
her- even after awakening from a nap
She was so mad- because she couldn't
understand the perverted secret shrine;
that went on under his thinking cap
And each time she got the chance to blow
a fuse; she would instantly snap
For she found him guilty of cheating,
yelling- she was sick of his crap
So she introduced his daydreaming face to a wakeup slap

And took the key to the car, cause in her mind- he took it this far
He blurted; she's worth more zeros than you can mentally count
So curiosity pushed her to ask; what's the amount
And sarcastically he stated- your entire bank account
He continued to stress; over his pride and joy
But she had a puzzled look on her face
With her eyes runny; like she was hit with mace
She boisterously wanted to confront the other girl
The so called center of his world
After she thought back to his comment,
on "her" being the investment;
she wanted to hurl
Not to mention her bowls getting loose
too; so she felt the need to poop
So all she could mention was – baby oops
And this was what happened; when
speculation caused her to snoop

Should I? Undoubtedly...

These days I've found myself growing more comfortable around you
Even more caring towards you
And stronger have my feelings escalated
Uncontrollable, are my passion and desires
These are my all-round characteristics toward you

But should I ... gain the strength that I feel; will help this
relationship out
By simply, sharing vital components from my past
Even though I want to skip the bad parts
No, I'd much rather keep it real
And just tell you how this brother feels

Should I ... let go and never try to grasp, relationships by the hand
Knowing that feelings do tend to form moving parts,
to a package deal
Or maybe, I'm just tripping 'cause honestly,
I won't allow myself to heal

Or should I ... just allow love to have its way
And just take a real chance, at being re-exposed to pain
Or maybe, I should make way for love's venerable feel

How should I ... ever be the same after being hurt
I blame the pain on this strong drug, called love
And why am I fool enough, to want to enjoy it again;
Undoubtedly, the future starts now ...

Not a complete mystery

They don't understand her
They think she's mean
But the person I know and understand,
they've never seen
And she's stunning in every color, I've ever seen, even in green
Darkness doesn't exist around her, 'cause she's a light beam
She's different though, but that's what attracts me plus mo'
That's why I'm not afraid to push down on the peddle and just go
She knows how to switch her style and look
Like flipping from chapter to chapter in a sophisticated book
She thinks she can't be figured out
But I watch her and study her like an elite scout
She's been hurt, 'cause the pain speaks to my heart, without a doubt
Well-guarded and contained, but emotions
spill onto my absorbing heart, like a light paint
And that just shows this attraction, 'cause the others can't notice
something so faint

In my dreams

She's more than a queen, in my dreams
I can see us dancing all day, until night impatiently overtakes daylight
We must be in heaven, 'cause we're both dressed in white
With you being present, my happiness has reached new heights

In my dreams the music that plays is perfectly conducted
It does as though it was instructed
No signs of it being corrupted
Playing free of skips and uninterrupted
God has us somewhere special, it's clear we've been abducted
It's just us two getting more acquainted with each other's mind
Not fretful about this unfair world, and it's people that are unkind
The best thing is, we're calm and comfortable, like we have tons of time
Holding you in my arms, I finally realize, that you're truly mine

Print in the folder

*I still remember where I met her; it was a freezing winter day, and
I was riding past the Desoto*
It was so cold that I felt as if I was in North Dakota
Her motions made her seem sad;
if only I could've stopped and lent her a crying shoulder
*I was admittedly taken away by her gloominess, and I yearned for
the chance to arrive home and pull out my folder*
*My unique folder, not only used for the means of verbally molding
her, but more like writing in it about her, and throwing all of my
hype in it*
*These fruitful words that aren't yet ripe, will mature be sent out in
hopes that she might one day take a bite*
*My words sent to you in many different ways, but all forming a
knot, ensuring that these words stay tight*
*As this poem finds its way to this young lady's heart, it shall fly
high, appearing to have the same elevation as a kite*
*When she receives these dear words that I've sent her, which acted
like a heater to her body*
More meaningful than the name Ed Hardy

Inspired truth

Everyday welcomes the next question to your test
Life's the teacher and it prepares you for your conquest
Situations arise to bring out nothing but the best
Why give at all, if you're willing to settle or possibly do less
Stop being afraid to stand tall
And yes, fear may reside in the next step that may cause the fall
*But your actions thereafter, will allow you to know if you're in it
for the long haul*
*Steps backward are often included, remember, before you took a
giant step you first had to crawl*
*It's all a part of the learning curve, you know; if you can't recall
you're retained*
Remember the saying, sometimes there is no gain without a little pain
But persevere and sustain
*Life's the ultimate circle; sometimes you go around, just to uncover
where you went wrong*
And the multiple trips is what makes the journey seem so long
But don't sweat the physicality, 'cause you still get a gift
And it all comes in the form of a much needed – uplift

Lifelike

She said that she was pissed,
so I instinctively thought back to our earlier kiss
But wait – was the kiss that dense?
I thought to myself, on how this made not a bit of sense
Found were emotions that drove me to become very tense
Inside, I felt a rising argument getting ready to grow intense
At this point, her heart was reminiscent of a barbed wired fence
So – like a wise brother, I remained stealth,
as I waited for her to express herself
After a while she spoke up, stating that she was just fed up
At this point I just listened with my head up
She expressed a distain, for work intruding into my personal life
As she continued to talk, I thought, only my wife…
Huh, was the only word that I could think to say.
And tried to explain how my job was well on its way,
to a very satisfying pay
She then looked back at me, in a puzzled sense and smiled
That's right; my girl smiled
But it only took a second till it flipped into a fiery frown
She then stated that something had to give
And all I could do, is think we still got to live
So we compromised and I took a much-needed vacation
She then pulled out a folder with a ton of Disney information
I thought to myself how crazier could this day get?
She answered by challenging me on the Play station

U

Rainy days …
Sunny days …
he's constantly thinking of you
A growing boy,
nonstop thinking of you.
August made two months since,
he'd last heard from you
Time open his eyes to more things,
he had to learn about you
Torn between a painful past and a dissatisfying present,
hoping for a paradise like future with you
Being no longer in denial, he had no reason,
to lie about loving you
Every night before climbing into the bed, he said a prayer for you
As the winds blew their paths become even more uncertain
He wished the best for you
If they never got involved in a relationship,
he would still be here for you.
For the first time in his short life,
he'd actually become afraid of love and lost at first sight

Strength & Beauty

She was beautiful and noticeable as a sunrise. But he, on the other hand, was as put together, and toned as a mountain. She sung with the power that could set your soul on fire, but at the same time, her emotions got the best of her showing she wasn't perfect. But despite her weaknesses, he had the ability to write with a passion that could penetrate the reader's heart, but at the same time his hidden demons sometimes resurfaced, giving him problems with trust and love.

With both her and him traveling from different directions, how would it ever be a possibility for these two individuals finding a common ground?

Strength and Beauty

She had a past which featured a couple of ups and downs, in which made her the complete lady of today. But the future she dedicated to pursuing and accomplishing her dreams.
He had a past which featured hurt and much pain, but a future which featured lots of promise.
Her smile could light up a room, and his somewhat of a smirk could only fit his personality.

What type of similarities could these two share, if both had so much that was opposite of each other?

Strength and Beauty

The first time his eyes were ever guided towards her, it was because of her angelic voice. Her voice had such an effect on him that it touched the hurt and the pain that he was experiencing in ways never before felt. He communicated through written words and she through music notes; little did they know, this was about to be a journey that would change their lives 4ever.

Enter the next horizon

Victimized by an unforgettable dry spell, that abruptly fell
This particular day's weather created a different tale
Through every act, the lessons learned, become critical facts
Life experiences lends information, allowing you sometimes to retract
And the unheard warnings often causes large numbers to subtract
Sometimes these are the consequent acts, of ill-advised flirting
Your own discretion can be a detrimental cause- of humanized hurting
Use your brain and find it imperative to think
In the long run, you're positioned, not to sink
Be prepared for whatever weather that could be at bay
In tumultuous weather, there's still hope that brings a brighter day
A little faith is that generator that makes everything okay

Unique vibe

A torn page from our youth; this is the whole truth
Written in text confesses the proof
I wouldn't lie on, I'll simply vibe on …

Love can be very nerve wracking
Emotions have symptoms; they're funny acting
We had lovely days, only to turn and be tested every other day
So prideful, couldn't follow my gut, and just obey; things would've been okay
Most days were so distinctive and memorable; that I wanted that back
The way we had each other's back, was pure love at its finest- that's a fact
So immeasurable, and beautiful was this connection, don't you recall that …

A torn page from our youth; this is the whole truth
Written in text confesses the proof
I wouldn't lie on, I'll simply vibe on …

So vivid in description makes for a part two within itself
I prayed you'd land where you belong, on someone's top shelf
This was when, I was forced to watch from the sidelines
Felt was the worst types of punishment, and the most trying time
I still can feel your indecisive heart, running in a race against mine

A torn page from our youth; this is the whole truth
Written in text confesses the proof
I wouldn't lie on, I'll simply vibe on
Until the vibe is gone …

I'll end by saying, Love is never lost;
nor does it grow old, but can always be renewed

Give me until tomorrow

Give me until tomorrow, that's what she said.
I remember because her touching voice echoed like a bell.
She was very ill and on her last leg.
Boy, all I could think was if time could move like a snail.
Her face was still beautiful but yet pale, and her body was beginning to look very frail.
But she was an up-kept virtuous woman; that you could easily tell.
She still continued to keep her wonderful appeal and fragrant like smell.
She truly preferred for me not to mention her well-being to anyone or tell.
But her last words were very lifting and would suit her legacy well.

Spring time Blues

O' Girl, how could this be
It's late summer, and I'm feeling a sense of early spring
You seem like newfound vegetation, in which I can't wait to watch grow
The lovely scent that you put in the air, smells fresh and sweet
Your company would be considered a privilege and a treat
You've opened up, expressing your feelings, in a manner similar
to flower petals
The feelings that often over take me, are starting to feel as if; they
are growing more settle
Having you by my side, would be like coming in first place, and
receiving that gold medal
At the beginning, I thought you were kind of mute
But those were the same qualities that made u appear more than
just cute
How 'bout we pursue a romantic endeavor; like a fancy restaurant
for two;
with yours truly sporting a suit.
At the restaurant you pick and choose, what you would like to apply
on the appetizer;
it could be Hidden Valley
It really doesn't matter; I'm not here to keep any type of tally
Allow me to pick you up, just to see that face glow and become smiley

No foreseeable end
(Dedicated to late Lady Carrie)

Never have I glanced my eyes upon you
I came two years after your painful departure
But my old man, thought the world of his bright shining armor
If image was everything; then nothing would've been able to harm her
She was known by him as his mother
She bore one son and many daughters, the five sister's only brother
The stories told of her; make heart's flutter
Your children's emotion tie together and hit home in a clutter
Grandma, your personality has been mentioned as being sweeter,
than honey butter
The true picture of a phenomenal virtuous woman
I saw the past through enthusiasm, that escaped each tongue
Your picture still ages gracefully, and the translation through your
young
You're more than a memory; even after twenty plus years, your
light is far from done
And the fact still remains, that you're compared to the likes of none
Your spirit and your images still live through your beautiful seeds
Noticeably sharing your traits, along with your unforgettable deeds
That's why you're still here, through your wonderful children
Still a present force, just as strong now as then with no foreseeable end

Sites in the (912)

I'm from a historic place in the South east
Sadly, some people cry in fear of there being little peace
But together we come, on account of a Thanksgiving Day feast
If not every enemy- family at least
This city is called the C-port,
In the malls the youth eat and associate at the food court
I'm still speaking of my home fort
On a street named victory, you'll see Hollywood looking palm trees
From time to time the pollen will cause you to sneeze
Humidity seems to own the weather
Some winters, you'll be grateful if you get to wear a sweater
You'll even witness some sad sights- like in the summer, crack heads rocking pleather
We're also known as the city by the river
Yep, a cool breeze off the riverfront could make one quiver
And engraved into our history is a fallen rapper named Camouflage
A memory that's hard for the city to dodge
The tragedy was pure pain
Left now is the fame in his stage name
I-95 makes us neighbors to Atlanta
The sport colors, red & black, no panther
Many Chinese joints, you get numerous tastes of China
And the Talmadge Bridge separates us from South Carolina

Don't 4get on this day

Don't 4get on this day … how your smile, let alone your knockout like beauty stands solo
And don't you dare 4get … how you're always standing at an A+, reaching 4 higher goals and never aiming 4 nothing below
Don't 4get that on this day … you're one step closer 2 being on your own, so don't try 2 speed up the inevitable; just take things nice and slow
And don't 4get on this day … how incredible and noticeable your all, around appeal is, which seems 2 let off this amazing like glow
Try not to 4get on this day … that some people could care less about your day; so let it continue 2 flow

Don't 4get on this day

But on this day, by the grace of God you will reach another age
Now you will open up your life's book, and turn to the eighteenth page
But don't take this new age and its newfound privileges 4 granted, because this 2 is just a temporary stage
I know you're probably thinking, that since you're now eighteen, you're finally being let out of your cage
But sometimes after taxes, your pay can feel like minimum wage
So do me this favor, and take all of this into consideration on this day

My hidden connect

*When we met; I was going through what seemed at the time as
unfamiliar tendencies
Back then, it just seemed as if it was so much, that could really
hinder me
That was, until the day I was reintroduced to you
When I met you again, I didn't know how to take you, but through
you I quickly learned that I had a purpose
You turned out to be my third source of inspiration, only third to
God and my love ones
With you, I can now describe myself as being fully complete
Through you, I've learned to express myself to the best of my ability
Showing me a newfound sense of much needed humility
Nowadays, after years of being heavily involved with you, I can say
that I've learned to use you as a utility*

What if

What if I told you that you no longer had to cry
And all your stress and worries could be tossed and waved bye-bye
What if this universe was ours for the taking
Making this the beginning of a new awakening
What if the light turned into night and the crickets didn't sing
What if we traveled first class to ecstasy with angel wings
What if we connected the stars in the sky
Why, 'cause I feel that with you around the experience would be fly
What if the image was proven to be our zodiac signs
That would be inevitability's design
What if this was a year ago
And you were a Virgo
What if we fell off and got back up, I guess people would believe in Miracle Gro.

Hurt is on the lurk

Hurt may have introduced itself, the day I opened my eyes to the female in the plaid skirt
I just had to know this meek one- who wore the collared private school shirt
After all, friends is all I saw, but it got serious when we thought that it was safe to flirt
But a year later, I know what went wrong; I'm well, alert
I was once jocular, far from unpopular
When she came, the change came
I dropped the little fame I had, to become what some considered to be a lame
It's funny how things don't stay the same

However this severe pain is still lurking
These insides are torn and dismantled thanks to the effects of this hurting
My heart is parched and just thirsty for some sort of mercy
So much turmoil, I have brewing on the inside, but I release it when I confess
But truth be told, I'm gonna need a huge mop for this mess
Say hello to reality, the sun is brightly shining, making it hot
My universe is cloudy and polar cold, making this fantasy real and my very own spot
It's hard surviving when you have half of a heart; I'm an emotional time bomb, but I'm missing a lot

Sometimes I wish these feelings would stop
The healing process has to be better than this depressing drop
But hypothetically speaking, if this is the healing stage,
then it shouldn't be long before I get back on top
Girl it's no secret we have tons of history
But how it passed so quickly is still an unsolved mystery
The only thing still noticeable is my familiar smirk
But since those days hurt has been on the lurk

On my behalf

You can never be hit with an eclipse
And your outer beauty 2 me, is only a glimpse
A sincere individual such as you, I've never known
To keep your name confidential, I'll just call you Ms. Almond tone
When I first viewed you, you stood under a spotlight and alone
Putting a young cat out of his cool and mellow zone
If ever God created a beauty as astonishing as you, I pray that you
stand without a clone

I love how your overall presence makes me feel
And please allow me to assure you, that everything I'm telling you
is real
Your spirit is harder than any blow, I've ever felt before
To avoid feeling twisted, I try to remain strong, but my feelings
ask 4 more

At first I was just after friendship
But my agenda changed after I heard that emotion, spoken from
your enticing lips
I didn't mean 2 sound sexual on that line, but remember I'm a Scorpio
You can even deny me if u like, but I had to let go and let you know
So this was to you Ms. Almond Tone, 'cause suffering I hate 2 see
you endure
And this is the truth no dishonesty- listen to my heartbeat its pure
But I'm not trying to rush you my way, but if necessary I can be
your heartache's cure

However, if u ever need someone 2 understand and comfort you,
I'm that guy
And there's no need 2 ask why
It's hard to open the windows to your mind without a lil draft
But you know I'm being open, like Moses did the red sea with his staff
I'm as serious as one + 1 making math
Girl don't laugh
Understand this was given to you on my behalf

Spoken truth

Let me in magazine J-E-T and you can call it a B-E-T
My rhyme scheme has a trademark flow
It's ancient like soul glow
My goal is to put the reader in a state of shock
Making my flow hard to mimic or mock
I have a style created by God, I must rock
The delivery puts a lump in your throat, similar to an Adam's apple
Try to wrestle with it, it's hard to grapple
My mind is leaking, but I go without stitches
I go hard like the 4ᵗʰ quarter; down 4 and inches
Each of my words has a job like the original members of the dream team
I spoke the truth since the age of fifteen
That's why my senses stay keen
Obey my warning- like my name is Hurricane Floyd
The words harass your thoughts and make you paranoid
Only because the truth; you can't avoid

Question about the game of life?

If life was like a basketball game I wonder what type of role would you play

Would you be my coach, being that I often listen to your words filled with promising outcome

I wonder could you display a court presence, like a point guard an uplifting vocal leader

Or would you be the dominant center on the floor, the one whom I look to for those hard points in the paint

Would you be my goalie in soccer, the one who teaches me how to block all of those negative comments, kicked my way by the opposition

Or if this life were a physical game of football, what position would you play

Could you be my brilliant offensive coordinator, which would help me break down each defensive blitz; rushed my way each week

Or would you be my flashy quarterback, running and throwing me encouragement every time you got a chance

See the reason why I asked, is because it really doesn't matter what position or role you would play, being that I would thank God for you just being on my team

Rational Thoughts
(Beauty of the Dove)

You begin asking yourself, what's so beautiful about a dove?
You then see attractiveness for the first time and want to embrace it.
Your insides start to tingle and butterflies take flight, you're now affected by it.
Your habits are controlled by your emotions- so you now notice it.
You can now, tight walk the sliver lining in the sky, you're now feeling it.
You momentarily have happiness but soon blow it.
You then grasp how precious every minute is; you now understand the importance of it.
The opportunity once again presents itself, so you know you must seal it.
You can now explain love and any question you had concerning it.
You were once broken, but now you're rebuilt, you now know why fools fall in love.
After these rational thoughts; you go back to your first, and there you find the true beauty of the dove.

Reflection of yesterday

We missed your birthday in December
This, I'll always truly remember
There was no room for just any lady,
being broken was the start
Tic-toc, tic-toc, was the sound of the
nearest clock; playing with my heart
Honestly no lie; non-stop
I was finally caught,
victimized by unforeseen thoughts
To live at the top- creates some addicts
Whiles falls from the top- feel so dramatic
The truth can be controlling, like sipping body shots
This definitely, wasn't my quick stop- or go to spot
But the pain wore on me like an interior wound
I tried to rebuild, even as life continued to resume
But there was only one loop,
that made it easy to recoup
So I had to find away to confess
I disbarred the stress
And found a way to digress
Thanks to this writing,
it was suppressed

Hypothetically yours …

Know that if you were mine;
I would value you better than time
If I were able, I would open up the clouds above
A light beam would cast down displaying who was loved
This would be on a nasty and rainy day
'Cause in a turbulent storm you would be okay
My desire for u would act as building blocks
Tied within the fabric of time, tighter than dreadlocks
Our foundation would be very grounded and settled
Stronger and more proven than any known metal
That would be the bond,
that causes all actions to respond
Actions would be tossed outward and beyond,
only spreading like ripples in a pond
You would be catapulted onto the notorious cloud nine
And we would vacation there, away from civilization's find
Together you and I, would be sky high
Looking forward, and turning away from premature goodbyes
In heaven we would appear, disregarding vanity and earthly fear
Freshly prepared grapes for my lady
Allow me to feed you, baby
In our newly acquired space,
we certainly dress in taste
Girl you look vicious; and most definitely delicious
I call it incredible and edible white
It's marveling eye candy to any sight
As I view you in your shape- revealing skirt
One of my body parts has a growth spurt
Maybe it's the seductive split on the side,
that has me wanting to tour guide
My thoughts and actions no longer willingly hide.
So my curious hands no longer abide
Things begin to happen unplanned

As actions birth reactions, that aren't hard to understand
The mental love-making, would not be mistaken
It would be higher than a climax
This could be too potent, but it's all facts
I take you from shy to your untapped max
You try to tighten up your body;
I whisper something both good and naughty
As your mind receives the beneficial fax
So you now comfortably choose to relax
The rest is poetry in motion- as our bodies' just act
I leave you lying on cloud 9ine in your birthday suit
Sipping on the juice of some unfinished passion fruit
You smile without saying a word,
But my actions went heard
At this moment I read the dialogue of a mute;
and it's unexpectedly easy to compute
We just took off! And we're still aloft.

Dedicated to Michael J. Jackson
(1958-2009)

Owned the moment

In "58" marked the birth, and in "09" marked the tragedy
Year "84" ushered in victory
Only to continue, memories that will last for more than a century
His dance moves were more like anointed
"The king of pop", he was crowned, entitled, and appointed
For almost half a century he owned the spotlight and a stage
He gracefully and fluently sung like no other, even with age
With a single sparkling glove, he grasped entertainment, and lead the Jackson 5
This man used it all: charisma, ability, vocals, and that much-sought- after drive
He started a whole new "Pepsi generation"
Bringing love through his occupation
Proving that it truly doesn't matter if you're black or white
Never succumbing to the stardom, or the legendary height
Instead, in a humble manner, he and his custom jackets shined bright
For many fans- this man was much more than just hype
They looked at him as the ideal, hero type

From decade to decade, and on through- the world viewed this phenom, as Mr. lights, camera, main attraction
Known for how vibrant he moved, and judged according to his uncanny actions
This man changed periods into commas
And united and diversified all genres
Seemingly never relinquishing his title or missing a beat
Even after death- fans will never allow his momentary touch, to suffer defeat
Remembered will forever be his many different styles – and his mystique
He was the 80s "Thriller," that "Smooth criminal", and the artist that painted canvases with his feet
He owned his moment

Something special

That's what I entitle this
Simply for you, miss
I still harness the feelings from our defining kiss
Despite our present tense
We'll forever be a smooth surface with no dents
From the first time we stood beneath the whole moon
To every time thereafter, in which I couldn't
wait for the excitement to resume
You understood me for the most part; and whatever
my actions you didn't fuss or point
To the beginning of a goodbye inside of a fast food joint
Memorable will forever be how you
broke my dislike for Valentines
And how on that remarkable day we weren't
official, but you still felt like mine
Taking us to another level; clearly notifying
some kind of apparent sign
Harmony is what we had
Despite the small things you did that made me mad

Conversation brought forth the problem and things
went from being moody, to being grateful and glad
We were all the way live; no commercial
You allowed me to just be me; you figured out that
I performed best, when I had no rehearsal
It was like we wrote our own book, like
chapter two sharing dinner
Each time having me feeling like a winner
Chapter three being in a little secluded
area by the water; star watching
Life seemed very in tune, as we listened to its
beautiful music; and kept marching
Chapter four saw me throw you; what you
called your best Valentine's Day outing
This particular day had my creativity; peaking and mounting
Something special was how we went upward and
came down like water from a fountain

Lip gloss

So clear that it's obvious, she's wearing it; or more like she made it
That's how much of an understatement it would be, to say it made her
So vivid, that she couldn't mistakenly be a blur
But more like excluding everyone else, because they were
Sculpted were those gorgeous lips that glistened
And her style spoke out to me like a recorder, as I listened
With an unmatched appeal, I had to wipe my eyes to see if see was this real
And before I could close my eyes to do such; her next move became too much
She got close with confidence,
and without a physical word- chemistry spoke that neither party was tense
And boldly without hints, I continued on present tents
Thank God, I wasn't out of my element
When I delivered a well-deserved compliment
In a fashion that was, first-class sent
I allowed myself to study her convincing lips that never lied
They showed the truth, like the mirror that had nothing to hide
These lips displayed beauty, first hand through smooth untarnished kisses
The twist is I'm speaking of, my misses

Writing on ya heart

Most call this writings on the wall, but I'll simply call this writing on ya heart.
I dictate my message to you, like only I can do.
For the world to see, the surfers, or even ya crew.
I'm addictively lethal, like a 3hird degree love burn.
I love the contact so I make sure that every hug is firm.
Yesterday you stamped your message, so today I take my turn.
Every word I give comes simply because it's what you've earned.
You're mine.
So why look forward to the 2econd month, when you're more than my valentine.
I could continue this for days, but I saw my hourglass, and out run my time.
So out I go, like open heart surgery; just to give you my heart to sign.

Day 2 day

Day 2 day based primarily on my shaken foundation
Changed every day by my situational circumstance and its many variations
Loving the one you're interested in each day; shouldn't feel like just another occupation
Even though it involves human relation
Relationships, do their best impersonating act of numbers, mathematically
And these days my words translate my thoughts radically
Ready to take my rightful place, so be brave when you battle me
Walking a bit colder after each fall, these are true words from my mouth
Born deep in the treacherous south
Sometimes I just call it how I see it, with no huddle
I learn to unconsciously step through each puddle
Which my tears produce with the passing of each fear
Question; which should accommodate my eyes, the future or the rear
I finally take my foot off the gas,
'cause the pauperize has finally decided, that it's no longer cool to harass
Driving solo, I told them I wasn't that entity that always wore a halo
But they still confused, 'cause my lyrics light but thick, like mayo
I loved her, no I still love her
Like no other, but that doesn't explain why I had to run her
We exist in the same place, but call us two different masses
But we're in God's rotation, so we'll end up wherever God casts us.

Retrolistic

Taking back by time, on this day things go in reverse
I'm talking way before Sprite was the drink to quench your thirst
Before life's meaning became an expensive dollar
I'm talking when it was cool to purchase,
dress shirts with a butterfly collar
Before fans looked at Michael Jackson in an outrage
Fans couldn't help but be mesmerized by his incomparable
moonwalk, across Motown's grandest stage

I'm talking when the Steelers ruled the 80s
When Iron Mike was putting grown men to
sleep, like they were merely babies
When Deion welcomed the name Mr. "Prime time"
When house parties were jumping off with Kid & Play
I'm talking mixes, from back in the day

Before the ice in a brotha's mouth, gave the viewers chills
When Philly had a funky fresh prince named Will
Before hip hop music became copycat beats and
lyrics, or sampled for a modern-day hit or thrill
Long before hip hop died or was killed
Way back when Mc's had straigh8 original
material and articulate skills

When Dougie Fresh was an incredible bebop machine
When most artist flows had strong intellect,
But the songs still reigned supreme
And they did this with lil to no profanity, I'm
talking when it modeled humanity
No style was farfetched- like slick rick and his famous eye patch

Or the emergence of a young teen, doing what he loved for pay
I'm referring to the Kango rocking L.L. Cool J
The saying was, sick, fresh, or even insane
But no matter the different mottos, one stayed
the same; stay in your own lane
It was clear, being your own person was essential
Like a young brotha calming to be presidential,
hint; Eric B. for president
Featuring the hip hop's human highlight film, Rakim

This era introduced the gold chains and Gumbe fades
With the deep part on the side, like every individual had it made
And before you had a CD
It was a cassette, and your Addidas- ask Run DMC
When the brothas wore the huge afros- with
the black fist picks; with the iron tips
And the sistas wore the afro puffs
No bluffs
Only to later have them activated, to birth the jerry and S curls
On the dance floor, grooving to tunes like let me see you swirl

Introduced
2
Cool

I was born with something those other cats don't possess
It speaks to them without lips even moving, this I confess
All attention pulled my way like I've got other fellas impressed
I show a confident swag in my walk, from the way I'm dressed
My mannerisms are on another level, so the slang term they throw me is; I'm a fool
Older cats still harness it, but I fine tune it with a touch of the new school
I smell a scent in the air and already know someone else has the same tool
I look and feel sophisticated
Knowing that I have my own persona, it's unable to be duplicated
My style isn't your typical that's known as hood
In fact, to monkey see monkey do, it may very well be misunderstood
They wonder where to start, is it present in the walk
Or could it very well be a mixture of the Southern North talk
Is it the chemistry I have with your sight

Thanks for the compliment, but not quite
To a tall person it could be anything but my height
Activated as soon as I awake from bed
I can't even say it comes from the head
It's just action-based, like Simon said
That's why I can't hide it; from my stride
It's silent but heard a-loud, like I cried
I was presented to me like a scholarship; you can call it a free ride
It stands out bold like it's the big three: joy, love, and pride
It might just be, the fact that I have a certain type of distinction
That won't leave until my expiration or extinction
Mentioned to only be grasped by very few
It might just make a brother appear to be Mr. GQ
This thing I produce, I want to introduce to you, as cool

At this point

I can't speak for tomorrow
'Cause for all I know, it could be filled with sorrow
But I love this bright day
All in which begun; either a month or two after May
For her I constantly pray
Hoping this won't be in vain, nor will we allow this to go astray
Uplifting and spiritual words, is what we incorporate and say

She helps me take my mind off of loneliness
And the beautiful thing is that I see no lust- and smell no bliss
For her smile is like paradise
I tell you no lie, I'm being very precise
In dealing with her, I've found myself growing quite fond
But the greatest connection ever felt, is our bond
When she writes, it penetrates my heart and causes it to leak
But the vibe is what the world would hear, if together we let our words speak
And I've noticed that for her, I've got a spot that's soft, strong and weak
So around her I prefer to be a little outgoing, but more so meek
But fine is her spirit and demeanor, like grains that are wheat
That's why there was no problem, letting my pen dance on the sheet

No refund

I know there is only one verdict that I must await
This information I hereby validate
I can be your example; look at me as a book with many chapters-
I give you my every emotional state
Excluding from my vocabulary and feelings the word 'hate'
My thoughts are diffused at times,
but my complete pieces I consolidate
That's why I'm not joking when I say,
poetry is my estate
But I would never fix my mouth to ask for a rebate
Sorry this isn't an open discussion, it's not up for debate
Don't believe me, listen to your eyes and just wait

Mama my radiant sunray

From my cradle to the inevitable grave
You'll forever be the main reason for me being so brave
For months I was a part of your figure
You were me and I was you
Never once carrying a stingy attitude towards me
And for this and more, I remain undoubtedly thankful to you
Early on, I didn't allow you to have scheduled times for sleep
Not with me holding the title of being; your
restless infant who loved to weep
But as I matured I didn't depart from your
lessons–'cause they stayed in close keep
I could never believe the many tears, that fell
from your face on graduation day
But still, I have many more accomplishments, I still have to repay
I've seen those hurtful things that have made
you cry, but you never quit on me and that's
what makes life meaningful to this day
God has truly blessed me with a pure and radiant sunray.

Happy anniversary 23rd

It's that month again, yep, it's October
This day 23 years ago, you probably were medicated- far from sober
You ask me how I feel annually on day 29
This year I feel a little older, but none the less I'm fine
Just aging like you, gracefully, with time
You give emphasis on this day being mine, but we share these 3hree
years plus 2wo dimes
Girl I'm speaking of the day I arrived, changing your status and title
The job you've done for 23 years and counting has been vital
And for it I say thank you and happy anniversary, mother girl
You're truly my world
You made the commitment like the vows I do, and for it all, I love you

The Center piece
(Powerful connection)

Give a hug, never take it back
'Cause it's a simple statement and act
It's all a bit mental, at times even sentimental
Like throwing out a meaningful kiss, if you wish
'Cause love is like a potion, containing much emotion
Together is how you must roll
Despite disagreements that may cause a short scroll
Through the thick and thin, to the very end
The ultimate goal is to consistently mesh
And for two individuals to become one flesh
Got to keep it fresh and new
This one's an important insight and view
It's so easy just wait on the cue
Stay spontaneous when you hook up for a date
Better sooner than late
Don't spend tons of time in a debate
'Cause you have no control over time and it'll quickly escape
Give one another a piece of the other's mind
Deep in the brain, is the discovery of the ultimate find
Lose the pride
Or be prepared to lose the beloved ride
Learn from others' mistakes, allow them to be your tour guide
'Cause the truth doesn't lie or hide
Properly introduce your significant other
Or trust they will, when they're involved with another
Don't degrade or make decisions based
on the fact that you're afraid
Keep your ears open, to constant things the other needs to discuss
Respect one another; there's truly no reason to cuss and fuss

Simply agree at moments to disagree, and
allow things to be argument-free
Don't settle; for that outcome has no mettle
And never become hostile or overbearing,
but stay loving, sharing, and caring
If you know an artistic way to show how you feel
Present it; just so long as it's from the heart and real
Constantly groom that unstable behavior, and
pray and leave the rest to the Savior.

The color defect

Drifting ever so gently alone
Sent from "The being" that holds the almighty throne
Through the complicated elements it blows
Where it will lose all motion and rest, no one knows
From heaven's door way a colorful snowflake has taken flight
But its looks are puzzling, you can only describe it as being
enchanted and bright
Others wonder and look from a whole new sight
More colorful than a kite
Something so beautiful it'll light up something so dark as night
It's a simple matter of error in 'cause and effect –
which created this color defect

Transformation

Yesterday I was a young caliper, before life embraced me in a tight cocoon
Yesterday I was at peace inside my new shelter, before my flesh received its first wound
But this day I take a second breath, as I escape with wings like an angel
But wait have I died- and gone to heaven?
No, I'm still on Earth, oh my
As I learn to us my God-given gifts, I will just fly
Not knowing where the breath of my savior will blow me
I just elevate and fly, leaving behind old situations that had me bound
But I now give a painful smile, because I'm no longer one with this ground.

Changing of the guard

Someone please stop the track
And rewind the preparation back
Yeah, what we built was the fact
That gave birth to an accomplished act
But now we must venture out
and reestablish our own conquest
Like us both traveling to unprecedented heights
But taking different paths, like one sailing and one by flight
Who spoke of the end; no, we'll forever remain tight
Both of us on a whole new altitude like the moment something
feels so right

It's hard to imagine the team not together
for the next installment which could be the best
But I will push on none the less
Understanding that life's a game of chess
The goal still above me – elevation
The act still inside you, acceleration
Together still fully understanding it- concentration
Targets sited, the next generation
Without any question we both must go hard
So believe that neither of us will spare the rod
But this day marks the changing of the guard
On behalf of Lloyd's upcoming success, I say, thank you, God

Growing up

I used to want the sitcom life-style
But only because my young imagination was running wild
I used to feel like I sat in the rafters
Afraid to make laughter
You stood front and center
Appearing cooler than winter
I used to long for the attention
But it was a full-time job, your actions mentioned
You knew everybody and their grandma
Well, at least this was what everyone saw
I looked up to you
'Cause a role model was in my view
Your skills I tried to mimic
But you taught me to kill the copycat epidemic

Little girl

You are ... little one you are
You're the smile that intrudes any frown
You're too humorous; you're a comedian's clown
You are ... little one you are
So mysterious at times, full of wonder
And full of energy, you run through my thoughts when I slumber
You are ... little one you are
A true sweetheart; I will never forget you
Enclosed in the diary of my heart – is the connection we made when you were two
Little girl, in a perfect atmosphere I would give you the world
Even if we feel the same distance that separates the East from the West
Little girl, if you ever go lost somewhere in the west, trust and believe I'll make that my quest
You are ... little one you are
Shining brightly like a young star
Keeping every eye ajar

Changes

Some changes are great, and some are your fate.
So it really doesn't matter if today or tomorrow, you still can't set a planned date.
This meaning that it's impossible for the change to be either early or late.
The only thing left for you to do, is just pray for the best and wait.
But no matter how hard you try, sometimes you can't shake it because in order to survive you have to take it.

Changes

After the intense struggle through some changes, some will be stuck feeling as if they're physically lame.
But lots of people won't feel lame, being that some will be left feeling emotionally ashamed.
However, through the change that you could endure, you'll become either tamed or even famed.
But then again, there's always that slim chance that the change could have no effect on you and you could just be left feeling the same.

So always remember this positive note, through changes you can start something great like using it as a milestone for shining and defining you as an individual.

CHANGES

My kicks

Take the time to step your feet in my kicks, if you dare
You'll be forced to decide to what degree you chose to share
Taking the time to walk around with these kicks on;
you'll get familiar with many different stares
You'll soon start to believe, that good friends are very hard to come by;
So you better hold on to them like good shoe pairs
See I mean no disrespect, but it's a known fact that life is very unfair
All of this, you'll gain just by trying on these kicks; I declare
So I warn you, wear these kicks well and show them proper care
This will prove to be an experience that you won't forget;
being that it's hard to live life in someone else's kicks.

Notable facts

Ask me something simple
And you might receive a dimple
Ask me something natural
And you'll receive something actual
But there are things that are beyond my range
They're many things that I can't change
Like some relationships after a heated fight
No matter how much I may try with all my might
Due to the severity of the previous act
Life sometimes doesn't allow me to revert back
It's just an instructing tool, that's a notable fact

Like first nature

Read me like a musical note
Then cast your vote
Grasp me carefully like fragile china
Follow the sheet like a definite B minor
Read me aloud like a trumpets sound
Now silence the tone, like a mute telephone
Read me with funk, 'cause you know you own spunk
Now read me mellow, whether you're a lady or a fellow
Read me until it sounds right, so figure me out slow
Now put me all together, and let the poetry flow

On the rise, is a poet

I'm a poet ...
taste, touch, see, smell.
Packed words travel well
Proud to be a part of this glorified story book
So timeless is its existence, ever evolving in its look
I'm a student of its teaching, and touched by its outreaching
I have a fond appreciation, of its unique creation
Longevity, validated
Langston Hughes, sedated
Maya Angelo, educated
My thoughts- awaited
With my faith, I've made it
I'm a writer, created to excite her
I'm that guy, that's fly as a kite, sir
Spiritual peace giving, from God through his pastor
Braced by God, so no concerns for major disaster
I'm a strong African-American male, with a unique story to tell
Learning to master the right essential tools
Raised by a village, and always remembered this rule
Taught love and always remembered to pass it along
Anything vice versa, in my opinion is wrong
Equipped with an old soul;
and relentless towards my goals
Trying to cater to all comers including my peers
So through poetry, I bring harmony to their ears
And thanks to my rise, I'll never forget my earlier years

I'll toast to that

So you got talent
And your message is non-violent
I'll toast to that …
And you got articulate skill, backed by extraordinary will
I'll most definitely toast to that …

Trophy gal

She questions if she was born with a blessing or a curse
'Cause she's like a strong drink that the guys thirst
Like a rear jewel she was designed to shine
She's the in-depth description of all that's fine
Born to stand front and center, never behind
And she's a new kind of picture like H3d; to every eye including
the blind
So kind-hearted
The source of her beauty that never departed
But this is the one feature that most guys overlook
This lady carries her worth, noticeably like a textbook
Her aroma is even tasteful like a top cook
All she ever wants is to prove, that she's more than a great look
But the art of her complex portrait, just can't be shook
She longs for a piece of life's massive pie
But half of the time she's either hurt or denied, being left high and dry
How could she be so beautiful minus a good guy
Numerous times she's thought to question why
And her biggest fear is thinking that her blessing is a curse
That's the thoughts of her silent unspoken verse
The unstable dudes try to get in her possession,
Trying to diminish her value like a worn purse
Simply 'cause they see her usually as one thing
To them her worth and value is eye-pulling like bling
She's a bragging right, to their flawed sight
They use her for a launching pad, to stroke their ego higher than skylight
She's like a diamond ring, no proposal
And their actions cause detrimental damage-
like a tear in the torso
Yeah, she's the beauty queen, and the trophy girl
Living in a cruel opportunist world

Raw an uncut

Pt. 2

Welcome

Your brain processes thoughts like car alarms that go insane
They reactively and subconsciously call Christ's name in vain
People see themselves so highly; it's evident, they're vain
The intoxication makes for a nightmare, in which they can feel pain
Blood soaks into this Earth, like crimson teardrops creating a different rain
Siblings still killing one another, are the norm since poor Cain
Disrespect to holy temple is displayed- with no regard or shame
But since you can't defend the sin, really who's to blame
What would be the justification and excuse used if Christ came
When we don't know we're classified as dumb
But if exposed to knowledge, be thankfully welcome
Listening results in becoming whole; through denial you're torn
Don't be a fool, allow knowledge to be born
Each day this Earth grows colder, so in reality you'll eventually mourn
Resist from taking any judgment into your own hands, this I warn
Now from this point on, read with clarity and understanding and- welcome

R'tistic Essence
(The Essence of Art)

Without further ado, I give you the ultimate R'tistic view Page | 3
Serving you with a taste of the upper echelon
Actions color-coded on the key, 'cause the words and acts bond
The universal R'tistic language, continues to be illustrated until the final dawn
Concrete images are manufactured like a classic hit factory
And the emotion that is stroked by the brush is everything but satisfactory

Feel it in the air – it couldn't be accurately explained
It is truly that in which has continued to sustain
It's the chilled nature to the earthy color tone
And it can usher in more themes when the earthy color is gone
It's the whole outfitted look on a gesture
It's the read appearance of body language in the form of a lecture

It's the motion blended ever so boldly together to draw you an in-depth picture
It signifies and personifies the whole entire means of the mixture
It's the experience of the feel
It's what creates real

See the vibrant change that could spark a new effect, that's elemental
Hear the classifications of the value that makes it essential
Feel the ageless and timeless texture, which makes it appear monumental
Taste the atmosphere's dew that sets in on the new horizon's birth
Smell then exhale, the scent of untouched worth

Paint, draw, write, take pictures, quote it, style or cut it, and cook it
Just visualize like creative eyes that memorize
Then you observe it and simply modernize; for its actually life-size
Let it speak volumes, 'cause its development was extraordinarily wise
It's present even throughout the wind's cries
It has raised the bar to unchartered highs
So get in where you fit in, and use your talent to join in this exceptional design, known as the essence of art.

Therapeutic flow

My hands act as the ventriloquist
The verbs set the mood, so lie back and feel the slight mist
Just relax and vibe with the lyrical-made atmosphere
There's no need to fear
It's all on the account of your important consent
So distracted it's like losing track of where the time went
Hint, it's like an internal scalp massage
Creating the picture, can you see the colleague
Let the words pour free like oil
I promise they won't spoil

A vanity affair

You so momentary like ice
Gambling with life like it's a game of dice
So you better be ready to pay the price
But I prefer to live mines, like its paradise
So think once instead of suffering twice
Don't it sound nice
Meet the narrator, and your host
So travel with me as we just coast
Either marry me or divorce me; regardless – no prenup
I go deep; and let it rush to the tip-top; that's how I erupt
I'm a live wire; so my intake of gasoline has sparked the ultimate fire
Words never stagnate 'cause they run on, they're simply fragments
Believe me, no fairytale
I'm just spiting; but it feels like betrayal
Love vs. hate, so an emotional dispute is involved
Presenting a problem that must be solved
And from it the solution will evolve
Call it the hate-love relationship
First the foul tip, followed by the forgiven kiss of the lip
So apparently you wear your feels like a side kick, at the hip
Mentally I feel trapped; it's confirmed through my thoughts that agree

But my lyrics breathe, and vent I'm free
Don't answer; the best thing we can do is, agree to disagree
Sometimes this is just how I feel
Meet the reintroduction of another side of real
Like gimme that, what I just did was just steal-
your attention, like violating your pension
Now open your eyes to description
Like a frisking, no – more like a shakedown
Watch out for the take-down, no, this is just a breakdown
This is the truth, 'cause it happens in every town
Blue flashing lights and sirens, now you see the sound
The kid's just partaking, in his passion
Uncontrolled verbs have no ration
I'm simply basking
I'll beat you to it; now save your questions no need for asking
Perpetual mind jabbing, 'cause the lyrics are everlasting
Call it eye candy advertising
Remember the appeal has to be mesmerizing
And the words create the picture's horizon –
Got to feel it, 'cause it's tantalizing
She's built, so noticeable your neck is at a tilt
A simple smile got your confidence sky high, like a stilt
This is senseless, 'cause its entertainment's vanity show
And oh, this is what it sounds like when I turn on the radio

Once told

Mad shout outs to lessons learned in wisdom, a long time ago
Comment not on a thought, but off of what you know
No disrespect if this is how you live; I don't mean to step on no toe
But this is just what I've earned; courtesy of what I learned, so on and so
In the next chapter, I was taught not to say ain't
But it still gets used, like a complaint
And say no such word as never
Even if it seems to be so closely linked to ever
And don't state what you can't do
Just give it a try, and let that try be true
Keep one objective, never fold
That's the best underdog story ever told

The gossip scenario

It's like 'extra extra, read all about it'
Gossip gets out of the mouth like spit
You know the scenario and how it goes
All cons no pros
It's constantly awake, no snores
Equaling tons of up-roar

That's why she lay with him and then Tim
And now she's a pregnant mess, and very stressed
Judged as a fool, 'cause she can't pinpoint the culprit's tool
So word on the street is, it could happen to you

It's like 'extra extra, read all about it'
Gossip gets out of the mouth like spit
You know the scenario and how it goes
All cons no pros
It's constantly awake, no snores
Equaling tons of up-roar

Now comes the issue with him messing with the wrong type of girl
You know what type, the type that can change any world
This catch was far from a pearl
All he was after was some pleasure that could make his toes curl
But the consequences make him want to hurl
Yo, live from the block, it could easily happen to you

It's like 'extra extra, read all about it'
Gossip gets out of the mouth like spit
You know the scenario and how it goes
All cons no pros
It's constantly awake, no snores
Equaling tons of up-roar

Three blocks over lived Ms. Innocence
Naive they say she was; in a sense
She was hidden from sex education
So lost, was thoughts of protection
In return she caught a deadly infection
But thanks to the God; Ms. Innocence is a walking blessing
Now she's sharing her lesson

It's like 'extra extra, read all about it'
Gossip is a bunch of non-sense
Why run and tell something past tense
Go honor confidentiality
That should be the mentality
But in reality
It's constantly awake, no snores
Equaling tons of up-roar

Lion

Leaving no room for many errors.
Isolated by his bold unique characteristics.
Over passionate about every move made.
Never showing noticeable weaknesses.

I'm built like a young bold Lion.

My decision 2 Run

There are methods 2 my madness, 4 one I like 2 run
4 the simple fact of being that the faster I run, the more I start 2 believe that I'm in the same level as the flash
This thought ensures me that I can't be touched
When I build my speed and reach my peak, you can 4get me being "it," hide and seek
Never allowing any individual 2 touch me physically, emotionally, and even mentally
When, why, and how do I accomplish this goal
Well simply put, anytime I feel threatened I just run
I run 4 a while, leaving the time around me following in a steady-like pace
I just run, it's a must, leaving all worries in the dust
Sometimes I don't run because I like 2, but because I feel that I must
I just run, dodging all anxiety attacks
But when I stop running, this is when I must face the hard cruel facts
This is when I'm left feeling the strain, which also sets me up 4 the hurt and pain
Who's truly 2 blame, I'm the one who ran … so the point is quite plain

Lowest point

Alone in silence it's just thoughts of maintain
Yesterday has become a memorable thing of the past
I so wanted to quit; I felt life's poison
I felt desperate and defeated
With my body of work now gone
Things seemed to be tit for tat,
How uncompromising is that
With every laugh, came many fears; that formed my pointless bath
I was battered;
And helplessly watched others around me seem flattered
At my lowest point, dreading sleep
Running from the images in the dark mass that loved to creep
Hunted, wondering what else I was going to reap
So the night became my active life; ditching slumber
And instead staying awake watching the walls and the alarm clock's
numbers

A look through the vent

I won't gloat; but this is one of the most heartfelt things I ever wrote
If time holds the key to change,
and you're the product, which came about due to a past exchange
Life being looked at through the vent, will never seem strange
I allow my thoughts to become the sounds and views from the vent
Flashback with me as I take you deeper through the past tense

At a young age we seemed sensitive to the slightest touch
Due to the fact that we were accustomed to so much
Or maybe because we were sheltered, not knowing life's pain without
a crutch

I still hear it, the first and the last time hope left, as you cried
It was devastating to my role, creating a newfound sense of hurt,
anger, and pride
So out of uncertainty, trying to make things better, I hesitated and lied
That day pieces of both of our innocence died

I asked my brother, not to cry
But the emotions had already climaxed to a level above high
For the first time it was just us two, no age gap; just you being my
closest guy
So together we looked back on our recent life, and unwillingly said
good-bye

Meanwhile a vital part of our life; sat back indulging on alcohol
Seemingly getting pissy drunk; flushing his important role down the urinal stall
A strong man succumbing to sipping all his problems away
As his two boys grew astray
We moved forward feeling as if he divorced us
I questioning why I ever believed in the hurtful concept of trust

At any given time mom's tissue would show what it looked like to sob
Her eyes red; cause she was angry with my father for lack of his parental job
He stopped disciplining and started asking questions that were answered with a nod
Choosing to take a more unfamiliar settled approach, with sparing the rod
At this point everything seemed every bit of odd

Betrayal

You made for the appearance of a shadow
Also dressed in armor for every battle
However formulated in your scheme were perplexed ways of errors
But how was I supposed to know that you made for unseen terror
Shoveling my position of comfort, you dressed in colors like a pallbearer
But I held sympathy for her, like Greek mythology's Hera
I told you too many secrets, so you fed off my nutrients until you made me frail
You exposed me; time after time through new tales
But now I still smell the smoke from the aftermath, as I recalled what was hell

Mental murder

He stands being convicted by the mirror
Now he truly sees the man in the mirror
His eyes show him the ways of his errors
The ears on his face; replay, "nothing can tear us"
The image that stares back; causes his eyes to release spillage
He remembers how he and she were the
members of a once-proud village
This, of course, happens after he sobers down
Now he's left trying to stay afloat, before he chokes
His tears create an emotional flashflood,
seeking to cause its creator to drown
His thoughts were his accomplice; they slyly provoked
She eventually told him that she forgave him
But his actions caused separation, now he
doesn't know how to save them

Moon vs. Sun

Long ago a war waged between darkness and light
For the battle over the skies
The moon was the deceiver, whose face appeared as lies
Both had their designated times to rise
And both in their own way were inconsistent
Especially the sun when she chose to be resistant
Out of the two she was the most emotional, always setting the tone
All over the places, being the reason for a different time zone
The sun stood for the balance in life
It almost held the same comfort as a mother and wife

The moon so beloved and yet feared
'Cause of the near changes that resulted in the weird
His presence is never overshadowed
He was said to have caused environmental changes countless times
he battled
Due to the cause of the change, people called it the light that was
responsible for the strange
Like his appearance; and the beliefs that at times he would try to hide
But also the effect he had on the elevation of the tide
He wore many faces thus gaining the nickname – the master of imagery
Never once being measured accurately in symmetry
Many believed he hid his true identity and use smoke and mirrors
like a mask
Probably the least recognized out of the two, but he probably had the
hardest task

One alienated to only night with an entourage of stars
Yeah, he got a share, but it still appeared like he's from Mars
While his rival fit right in; and time after time raised the bar
Moon's envious relationship to Sun seems as dark as tar
But with so much of this relationship acquiring jealousy and deceit-
this dysfunctional love affair seems bitter sweet
Now the astonishing thing is that together, they form something
unique like a bloodline
But that unforgivable act of Caine and Abel is still unkind
These two can never co-exist in full appearance at the same time

Feel me
(Understand E. "Luv")

The flow is a part of my brain.
Lyrics are evident like a picture's frame
The journey is through my eyes
My upcoming is courtesy of the no quit in my tries
The gravel is one with my shoes
Trusting in God I will never lose
The love shapes my heart
But still it's a delicate part
My style is distinguished
I don't write when I'm anguished
I'm a gentleman that's recognized that he's God-made
I'm on a constant upgrade
I speak it now, so future wise, I'm gone to be paid
Unlike images in mirrors, I don't break nor fade
"Beautiful," your self-esteem was sliced; don't worry, 'cause I've got
your first aid
I got an "A" on my morality, and you can add a plus- to my Southern
hospitality
Why should I stray away from my principalities

Exploiting Couples

Are strong couples, defined on whatever they can endure as a unit
Can couples survive in a society filled with hate and envy
Or, are strong couples truthful and still often doubtful at times
Why are some couples often introduced, to forms of denial; when
things become heated
Or are some couples living a huge lie, and the only reason that they
still remain together; is because of the public eye
So how do couples, really and truly beat the odds; no matter what
trails they encounter

Exploiting Couples

See I must admit, some couples are living examples of what love
could and should truly be like
However, some couples only exist on infatuation and lust
But then again, many do exist on real love; and most of all trust
See, I do know that in order for every couple's relationship to work;
Love and trust are big must
Both individuals that make up the couple; should be able to bring
something to the table that the other can't
So now I ask, are the best couples the ones that never succumb to
obstacles, but instead, are the ones that are able to overcome them?

One accord
(Dedicated to Will &Tara)

Before me God has given you, as my richest prize
Beauty is within and without you, even present in your unique size
I have faith in your abilities, that's what I say if asked
You give your kind heart and soul, in the finished results in whatever task
Give me your hand- and together we can embark on a voyage of no return
And join me as together we toss individuality into a selfish inferno,
then watch it burn

Let's learn to be each other's stability
Because traveling this road that we chose- causes for joint mobility
Let's make an oath to live right
Despite living in a sinful world filled with hatred and spite

You make me feel the essential components, of being in love for real
And being with you has made me believe that, love has the power
to heal
The first man once stated that the first woman, was bone of his bone
So I say; let's come together and form an entire ribcage, until God
calls us home
'Cause being on one accord is our mission, regardless of the stormy tension

THAT'S WHAT LOVE IS

It was the hottest and most humid day during the summer, and I was exhausted with nothing but thoughts of failing running through my psyche. But to my surprise she spoke to me. She told me to continue, having an effect on me that was almost similar to a cool wind blowing and rejuvenating me. After I heard her voice, she gave a defeated young man a second breath with no more thoughts of failing but passing, and persevering.

THAT'S WHAT LOVE IS

I was in a sour mood and full of discomfort after a long night of having no sleep, and I just focused my attention on sleeping away tomorrow. But out of nowhere she spoke to me, stating that it's a time for everything and I shouldn't sleep so much, because while I'm sleeping someone else is awake prospering. Possibly even, becoming the next Bill Gates, all while I'm sleeping. After receiving that warm-felt message, I decided to dedicate the following trials and tribulations that I faced as being a rewarding opportunity for nothing less than the possibilities of success.

THIS IS AN EXAMPLE OF LOVE

A mother-to-be, finds out that she's in the fight of her life. With this in mind, every breath that she takes could be her and her baby's last. As the doctor whispers into the ear of one his nurses, he states that he doesn't think that there's a chance that both will make it out alive. The mother over hears this remark and tells the doctor that if her child has to live and she has to die then so be it. For the love of her unborn infant is overbearing. However, both baby and mother make it out alive. For you see. THIS IS TRULY WHAT LOVE IS.

It was a time period filled with pure evil and betrayal, and God was thinking destruction to bring about new results. However, unlike any other man before himself, Jesus stood alone and took the beating of all beatings in a lifetime, insuring that the sins of man were covered. Dying on a cross was the almighty task that he set out on completing. NOW THIS IS THE ULTIMATE AND NO GREATER LOVE.

I'm that radical

I may tell you that I'm a minute in time
And when I speak it's effortlessly; my mouth isn't confined
A thought from God I can't bind
I may even throw you a metaphorical stanza – that doesn't rhyme
But when you finally catch it and eat it, your face turns up like you
ate a lime
So we're different, it's apparent, but is this a crime

Maybe it's the truth that's hard to guard
I'm full of sought-after ambition
And I'm a Godly young man on a mission
God blessed me with divine intuition
But your problem is, when I don't entertain the negative tension
My apologies on that subject, some things are better unmentioned
When some are in a rough situation, they then want to use; a reliable
and trustworthy extension
What they refer to as lucky number seven, so they call up to heaven
Not understanding that this number is God's number of completion
This number was present all the time- it never underwent deletion

So why you call on God just for an outlet, when your life's in shambles
or standing still
Man, misconception kills
And I mean at will
That's why reality slaps you, when you run out of that green stuff;
you call the almighty dollar bill
Seems to me that you've got the world's philosophy
One being that God isn't the Almighty, and he isn't the supernatural key
That's why you continue to do, what you do best
Verbally spit bullets- but I got on God's bullet proof vest

Twisted is the world's principles, that's why the good sometimes get accused
See, I know that some will urinate on my views
And sorry – I didn't mean to amuse
Please excuse my passion; sometimes I speak like I've blown my last fuse

That's why I say forget, the so-called longevity of money
'Cause it's the main reason so many act so funny
Not to mention it being the reason some people's eyes stay runny
Instead – I say give me some Godly loving that's sweeter than the best honey
But maybe the truth lies- in thoughts that seem too practical
See God's going to allow my mind to multiply like numbers, it's all mathematical
And as for the world's perception of me, well, I'll just continue to be known as a radical

Speaking to you

The responsibility of defining a man is now on
Being that the daddy's no longer home
So you're a young man feeling on your own
You wonder -what's the correct path
When truthfully you don't even know half
Internally you question how to respond to experience-
when the facts classify you as a calf

Denied proper nourishment, so stunned was your growth
You became your own definition of a man, and advice you treated
with loath
The fight is to make it, by any means necessary being your M.O. and oath

So mistake-bound he clearly was
Quickly creating the wrong kinds of buzz
Give your growth a chance to evolve with time
And use your wisdom as a resource, and your mind
In doing so you will be creating and establishing your own mark
and line
Trust that, constant growth comes with a notified image or sign

Human I am

Human I am, which doesn't shield me from the verbal lashing
However they lose their minds, because my truth is harassing
See my lyrics, try 2 understand my rhymes
Feel my passion, get acquainted with my poetic style
My black and white fashion could still be considered dashing
But unique like the lines in my hands, is my very own passion

Human I am, which allows me to lose it and snap
However they lose sight of me- if I'm resting in their lap
I refuse to be slept on- I keep it untapped, cut the crap
Feel my passion, face felt like you just got a pimp slap
My black and white fashion, is a nightmare in your nap
But unique I am, like a world compass on your map

Your choice
(I am man)

I get overwhelmed and search for happiness in the wrong realm
I fall to oppression and others witness my unattractive state of depression
I feel an inner pain that brings anguish
Longing for an companion, I meet drugs and find there hard to relinquish
So sadly they take over my world and I become vanquished

Now I'm under the influence of ... I've even forgotten how to love
Feeling high octane or more like anything other than being sane
With little sense of reasoning or moral, confrontation is coming I can't reframe – spending my money on the wrong things I blow it on another whip
Like a newly pronounced father, I tote concealed iron tips
Just the thought alone makes my adrenaline do back flips
But I become offended for being apprehended
Thank God for stopping me before another life was ended

I finally awake and can acknowledge that I was wrapped in sin
And understood that this world didn't self-produce this poison
I also understood that when I was caught there was no one to fault
Sadly I had to go through these events in order for a lesson to be taught
Through it all I'm built Ford tough, no my mind is hard like a boulder
For my lady, I should've been willing to lend my shoulder
I am man and I pick this day to take a dramatic stand
I'm solid like a body of land
Positively working diligently with my hands
But my mind is my enemy
That's how the devil tries to hinder me

I become the target with a little color to my face
And if I speak my mind my eyes taste mace
Some things can be avoided, but I got an attitude like this world's
on my case
I'm still living a nightmare, 'cause I still feel hidden inequality undercover
I have multiple baby mothers … 'cause I have a problem with trust,
courtesy of lust, yep … twisted were my priorities
And I constantly wondered why so many people, were statistically
considered to be a part of different minorities
I am the voice of a certain type of man, but open for your discussion
is your choice

Bodies of water
(Dedicated to the diversified woman)

Women are like bodies of water
Few are like the very pools men created; shallow and easy to
view the bottom
Some rest in a secluded manner like puddles,
that are settled
And some methodical and steady when they maneuver or speak-
resembling a flowing creek
And some are naturally determined to make it through any seam;
like active moving streams
Others act as rivers, that flow steady, being opportunistic and ready
Some fear their next move, so they settle into the state of a pond,
always rethinking what would've happened if they just would've
went on and beyond
With some, simply the next move depends, thus creating a gulf
which are enclosed by their friends
Some are independent and considered to be great like some lakes
And at last, when they reach or overachieve their goals, they evolve
to a place free of boundary
A massive new body, full of diverse surrounding cultures, it's the
greatest exposure
This ultimate body inherits new motion, for there is no other body
like the mighty ocean

Recharged

It's like I see the world outside of my garage
I avoid being hasty and reckless, so I don't barrage
I've got to stay humble, 'cause I'm not in charge
And in return my thoughts are enlarged
It's good to receive a recharge

Feared ending

Their mouths are venomous like the most deadly snake
Their mind is a loose wire
Their word preference, is like an electrical fire
Their heart is crisp dark, only 'cause their oven is set on constant bake
Turmoil is in their eyes, that's what you'll always see when they're awake
Scorched and torched are their limbs 'cause they've already traveled in hell
And their tickets they preorder with spares, and deceive with words like you didn't get this from me, but it's wolf tickets they sell
The burning of their own ashes they can't even smell
They despise cool temperatures
Hopefully fire won't be their unfortunate demise

Her motto

(Me & C)
I slept walked for far too long
But why did I enjoy living wrong
A desirable routine, like a favorite song
The song skipped, before I heard what was truly said
Years, all I had were numbers hanging over my head
Like the repeated skip, the hand was delivered fist lead
What someone tells you, should be warning enough to run
A devastating reality follows the results, of what someone's done
I reflect on the jeopardy that surrounded my son
God forbid the worst, and the psychological damage being done
Many may never come clean;
but hidden were gestures obscene
I know some viewed me as stupid
However, I simply wanted to, delete Cupid
But we strategically strive and survive; and live to evolve
Now, it's my lil' man, in which my world revolves
I effortlessly cast my worries to God, who problem solves
As I begin picking up the pieces, the taste is bitter sweet like Reese's
Piece by piece;
is an acquired morsel like quiche
Life is becoming fulfilling;
I'm refurbishing and rebuilding
No intended disrespect, as I reflect
I can no longer neglect,
my goals and standards are now select
This makes year three, which I'm drama-free
What comes next is key; you don't have to agree …
Just please respect and learn the motto; it's just me and C

A warrior

Numerous times you've tried to steal from me,
what didn't even belong to me
So I say to you, your train of destruction has
been derailed
I call you a liar, and stand as proof that two of
your plans have failed
See you battle me but I'm like a robot,
my information has been plugged in from above
Showered down on me as thoughts- with love
In fact your actions have empowered me and become my fuel
I see how you deal, your motives are full of pain and cruel
Hell on earth is your objective for the world, that's why flipped
are the rules
But what I was sent to do is expose your plan, and send my Father's
children to school
This is way past flesh and blood; this is spiritual warfare, so land
can't be conquered in this duel
That's why it isn't much negativity that hasn't been heard
But tightly grasped should be the Holy Word
See this war talk I'm spitting, may be too complex for a certain
individual
That's why if you want to battle along side of God, elevate your ability
and become a warrior that's spiritual

Pain

Pain is our imperfections … and pain shows developmental
progress
Pain can have you feeling a total mess
When we feel pain … we truly feel the strain
Pain is nothing more than a seen and unseen wound
that time must heal
Pain is actually more than what we feel
If pain, never properly heals, then pain will evolve
And when this happens it becomes a legion … and that equation
is hardest to solve

Purity

The picture is painted in the color white
Made of an element that's unmatched
Even called a radiant ray of sunlight
One word classifies it "New"
Never used before, so it's far from old
When you are pure you are one of a kind
A gift from God

"You Only live Once"

I do what I do; when I do it
I do it fast, or I do it,
like some versions of the music;
and chop and screw it
It's none of your biz what's in my cup
Just know it does its job; and help me erupt
Afterwards, I get straigh8 to it, when I parlay
I long stroke who I may and call it a momentary short day
'Cause when it's night time, it's bright light time-
and I go out to play
I'm the life of the party; even if I have to bring it to the lobby
I still have wishful people from last encounter,
waiting in hopes for a sorry
I'm just having a ball like Mr. Sheen, or simply Charlie
The ladies want encouragement, so I help with a tip;
as overdrive becomes their body
With that liquid courage in me,
I never know who's about to become my momentary shawdy

I wake up, and think on ways to get my cake up;
and by night's end, comes the shake-up
I turn down for what …
I may even be guided to slap a girl's butt
I hear the concern in some of my family's voice
But I do what I want, according to my choice
They whack anyways, I'm just living my life nowadays
I just enjoy myself, by constantly going dumb
But the ol' heads say, I'm just young dumb and full of cum
I do all phases of fun, to the max …
just ask …
A threesome including me and my hun
And three this time, makes next time an additional one
But for all the fun in the world, consequences make you grow,
and disregard the greed and more
So I've finally had my share of negative tours
Yeah, you only live once, but child behaviors are a part of a stage,
and accountability later hunts
Oh, to be up so high, just to get dropped so-low
Makes for nightmarish thoughts of the saying "Yolo".

Lost in thought

Roaring thunderstorms reside in the inner portion of the mind,
that somehow become surreal
From the storm I out last the flash floods making me without a doubt,
the real deal
My breakfast and lunch is knowledge that sparks an everlasting
hunger,
which I consume like a hearty meal
This comes with no denial over what I feel
That's why I roll this wheel
I'm like an orange; in order to reach me,
you got to go through the protective peel
There's no longer laziness in me at night,
I go to that secret place in an unconcealed kneel

Mz. Emotion

I must introduce you to my other half
She's my strength; she's my substance; she makes me laugh
She must me a female, because she's dictated by feelings
All senses tied into one, sometimes generating unique healing
She dresses to impress, in what some may think to be a bit revealing
She's a bit raw
If powered by anger; don't let her catch you with her lobster claw
She's priceless; you can't calculate this gold chain
Her actions are drawn from her unanticipated brain

Full moon

Bold as a heated attitude.
All out in the open
Steadily, its shape is reshaping and redefining.
Always responsible 4 noticeably shining.

Your share

First let go of the keys to your cage, and be free
Don't knock it till you try it, and you'll finally agree
Next be here physical, and not over there
Continue to follow me; soon my words will be made clear
'Cause their minds can be there, but yours over here
Let your thoughts remain rare
That's why I receive puzzled looks and constant stares
Once you understand you'll see, that different we are;
like the diversities of our hair
Just dare to be different, and grab hold of your share

The forgotten ones

This is a part of the unknown society of this large world
This place among all others do exist
But surprisingly, this is one of the few that are underestimated and
quick to be dismissed
Except for a tragedy, which in their eyes is glorified news they
constantly release
The blood-starving and thirsty media, looks at this environment as
an opportunity to feast
It's been nicknamed and called many things, but many refer to it as
the ghetto
Looked upon as nothing more than the bronze medal, and a place
chosen to settle

Also known as the hood which is never fully understood
Quick to be acknowledged for all the evil, but never mentioned for
the good
Normally showered in dismay
And society sits back and reacts rather slow, but we know this isn't okay
Cast out and often feeling abandoned all because of where they stay

Welcome to their world, where harsh realities lay claim
But for some, sports, intellect, and over-driven achievers still reach fame
Discovering new ways to change the game
This place doesn't make the people, the people make this place; so
understand their aim

Some are simply go getters; personifying what it means to lean not on tomorrow
These are the ones that refuse to lie in the rains of self-sorrow
But some teens break their moral, values, codes and virginities and think it's cool
Leaving many to believe that these are the hard knocks lessons that should've been taught in school
Statistics try to state that the young brothas are most likely to find a job on the corner trying to sling
But with the quick money, comes the wrath of the problem; like cops looking for the expensive cars and bling
This setup leads to the pin; on a varied wing

Society also witness the brothas helping make the babies; but leaving both the child and the young lady. But they'll help support Jordan and the shoe store
And the sista's get caught up in foolishness like clothes that they don't have the money for
Welcoming the persuasion to steal, as one door opens and the other closes for sure
Too often is this place mentioned for its negative over positive moments, more and more
It shouldn't matter if you're from the upper, middle class, or the ghetto's core
We together have to stop with the slander and behavior that's considered malicious
For there's no reason for us as a united and diversified people, to be so vicious

Rebooted

You can't hit what you can't see
You can't devastate me, if there's no I in we
You can't enslave someone that knows he's free,
You can't limit something- that's considered to be a poetic spree
And you really can't harm me
'Cause, it's an uphill fight that starts, below my knee

So to make this perfectly clear- I'm back
Never again toting an empty back pack
So check this, I want you to try to attack
'Cause the lord allows me to roll through any barricade stacked
And I'll also give you some ol' school advice; stop, 'cause your
attempts are whack
See, I'm not old and run down- like an old shack
I'm not even of this world, in fact
That's why some are simple-minded– forgetting that God's effect is
the total Impact
God's knowledge secedes all; you can't pay the world for it; it's not
on a shopping rack
So avoid the trouble 'cause you'll be rewarded with nothing, not even
a plaque

Dark ink

The SCPD is called for emergencies
But sometimes late, they arrive and faint;
too silent become the screams
You already know what that means
Detectives try and solve tragedies
Using methodical strategies
Trying their hardest to gather and sort
But the wrong person is sentenced in court
In a little city we call the sea port
Unsuspected relatives read articles
boldly until their lips get chafed
The suspect had no remorse … for the elderly-
so no age is safe
If a street runner makes it past twenty
he should be thankful for that
I look and read the city's newspaper
And it looks like reprints to be exact
With the death of a teen, retaliation is how
the squad reacts
Multiple homicides, no fiction or exaggeration
It's all facts
And hidden is one body, until it starts to stink
With hurt and darkness, attached to the dark ink

The Price

It strikes without warning; it's the most lethal sniper
Your cells are no longer good guardians; it becomes
infant-like, with no need for a diaper
You think back to your earlier actions, and
realize how you may have gotten this
Then you quickly become pissed
You remember stuffing the envelope and
sealing it with a special kiss
But was it all just out of lust and bliss
Well it's too late to dwell on the past now
And you're sitting there looking like wow
You're left looking at yourself in the mirror
And the story becomes even clearer
You slowly tear up
But now you have to man up
You reluctantly pick up the phone
But the phone just rings and you realize no one's home
You prepare as you locate the correct number to dial
Reality strikes, and you become terrified like a child
Meanwhile, someone picks up and just like
that- you have an appointment
You wish this was only but a minor cut, something
that could be cured by ointment
Truthfully though, you knew this was coming, just
never knew when this gift was going to be sent
These repercussions you never would've anticipated
If you would've known a head of time you would've waited
You begin to quiver, thinking on the
medication's cost; that has to be paid
But out of nowhere you think, wait, is there
really a price put on the head of AIDS?

War with self

First off I got a daily pending vendetta
Each day I pledge loyalty to the, side that's better
My flesh is the enemy
it knows me through and through,
even my rational tendencies
But I still fight on, knowing that there's a reliable remade
And I'm not thinking about a substance, so you can pour out the
Hennessey
'Cause if I listen 2 to my flesh, it can most definitely get me tipsy

The metaphorical image
(Side 2, type B)

Living within a complete state of solitude
Nasty, vindictive and isolated, is his attitude
Deep in the roughest part of his makeup, lies the hungry imprisoned lion
Relentlessly pacing and reacting to every movement
In his mind he illustrates a silhouette of dismay
For this very reason, trapped he must stay
He licks his dreary cave full of flesh altering fangs, at the thought of
being freed
On that day many bystanders will bleed
A dark trance-like stare, comes upon his face as he listens for the pleads
But he wants to detach limbs, as he treacherously feeds.

If I were you

If I were you I would divorce stress, so I could learn the meaning of rest
I would understand that each day presents a new test
I would take hold of God's hand and let him control me like human chess
'Cause my life is like the game on the board
And the puppet master is God my Lord
I would let him make life simpler and recreate,
knowing that I'll end up in a better state
I would open my heart to him and just romance
In return it's me he'll enhance
I've got to take a chance
Let him change my staggered slouched position, to an upright stance
After all, art was the start, so he'll eventually arrive with a camera
trying to freelance
If I were you I wouldn't give up on my Godly quest
And I wouldn't let someone rejoice over my current state, 'cause still
to come is my best
But this you really don't have to do
I'm just telling you the simple things I would do if I were you

So misunderstood

I come from the, savoring honey-making beehive
All wrapped up in history, like an archive
So off the wall, like Michael Jackson
Spontaneous are my actions
So not a part of "The System"
What are the true motivates of the so-called high ones – who enlist them
And yes, I was him, the one who was formerly about this and that
Not proud am I, about those particular stats
But I've truly learned from my acts
I'm not arrogant, just know I'm not a one and done
As long as I'm given the go from the Lord above, I'll shine like the sun
I'm all about the peace movement, but I'll still strike with lyrics that
weigh a ton
I sit and see things happen- rather slow
It's sometimes like seeing the wish you make- well before you blow
Crazy isn't it; it's like I'm living in once upon a time ago
Maybe I'm just ahead of the race- or maybe to others I'm cheating
'cause they can't keep pace
I try to stay straight laced and understandable- like a well written book
But even though I drew my thoughts out in my 1st book, I'm still
receiving salty looks
I don't know, maybe it's me but these food critics have to be the best cooks;
must be nice not to make mistakes
But they feast on my shortcomings, like they're delectable stakes
I used to hold back- but now I question why –
here's that much-needed sigh
I won't, can't, and will never settle, so I got to push that accelerated
gas peddle

The metaphorical image
(Side 1, type A)

Enduring a state of tranquility and peace
Habitual and more so steady, like the sun resting in the West and awakening in the East
Admired and comforting to his soul, like the sunflower that adores its main source of power
He looks high to his master
Even though he's rooted in a field of pastures
Forever vibrant, but yet extremely humble
On occasion he bends too, but his roots are strong so he doesn't stumble
He's even supportive, as he reaches out to graze
Silent is he, but still he manages to stand out everyday
He accepted his role to his environment, so he's rooted to his calling, but still he's free
His understanding for life is his primary key
And he shows that silence, is often an intricate part of the learning process

A cracked glass

My eyes grew bigger as I drew nearer
An unexplainable image I saw, soon grew clearer
My features through this glass spoke the truth of the matter
The glass was cracked but it didn't shatter
And for some odd reason, it wouldn't break or scatter
The image was very much distorted
Out of fear I even thought to abort it
But something in me still wanted to promote it

Psychologically, the image just wouldn't let me be
So I left it where it was, and thought to flee
But part of me wanted a second view, as my mind continued to plea
So I found myself staring back at this glass
I saw that my opposing counterpart had not a bit of class

where a once compete compact image appeared
I looked at it as though I was a physician, and noticed pain between the cracks-
the symptoms of hurt I feared
No longer daydreaming, I continued to stare, as I noticed that this was far from a nightmare
With every crack God showed me my harsh atmosphere
My image was damaged by judgmental views – and I figured out that they can't break me I'm still here
So I relived the harsh reality of being stabbed in the back
And quickly understood the different cracks
I understood the image from this point of view, and I could no longer see a blemish
Regardless of my so-called allies, chilling in seclusion trying to scheme and diminish
Little did they know, God showed me that he still knew how to replenish

2 Faces off

No more, anything he can do I can do better
Now I see we're complete oppositions, he's like lead and I'm a feather
He prefers doing dirt at night, I prefer doing good deeds no matter
if it's daylight
On sinking sand, he throws rocks and hides his hands- but on level
ground I stand
After years of chasing him
I finally face him
Eye to eye and nose to nose
We're set, to lockup
No longer am I a young buck
No longer does my head duck
I don't care if we do look a like
His picture is dark, and mine is light
This is the moment
No longer will I share it or loan it
So I must find a way to owe it
This is the intense face-off
Simply looking in the mirror no rehearsing
Truth wins despite first or second person

Not conformed

I'm starting to believe in things-
that don't coincide with this reality
And this world's sadistic principalities
See, I now believe that in this realm you're limited
That's what makes my thoughts irrational
But you can assure that these tips are factual
We live in a counterfeit reality, this is actual
Reality, huh, filled with so many that love brutality
Displayed on a daily, in the form of much physicality
I'm not conformed to this world
That's why I must let my spirit, determine the right girl
I've been blessed with a new set of eyes
'Cause this world, views and accepts the truth as lies
But stubborn and unworldly are their hearts,
that's why this vital organ cries
Some receive a perk from this world's drugs-
that gives momentary highs
But pain and strain is reality when they come down-
'Cause the after-effects chastise

Misjudged

Brah, I heard your silent cry-
that bleed out with every unplugged bullet hole
You were truly cut, out of an original mold
But by the time you passed-
misunderstood and controversy was the image that the world sold
But some-times we become our own enemy, and led our self down
the wrong path
So when this happens, sadly we have to deal with the inevitable wrath
But ever present still remains, your craft
Those signature pieces have stretched minds and caused them to enhance
You allowed young brothers to believe in poetry, and they gave it a chance
So the lesson learned was, to never fall victim to our own circumstance

A painful act

He stood as skeleton figure, due to the alcohol which tends to ossify
But he had to go through a strong state in order to detoxify
In order for him and his true love to reunify

Spirit felt

Blind anger tries to knock the door off the hinge
Sicken is the thought of revenge
It satisfies the flesh and makes my spirit cringe

2 whom it may concern

Watch your path, for one long eye blank;
and you can make the wrong turn
Fight through the fire that delivers the slow burn
No hard feelings; tough love teaches a memorable way to learn
You'll respect it more when you understand; what you have you've earned
Sometimes life presents a degree of seriousness, that questions your concern
But follow the truth and the light and remain stern
Keep your mentality sound and firm
And keep your motives clean, to guard against despicable results like a germ
Most times the flesh is rough and tough, but you have protection, call it Lubriderm

Staring in2 the unknown

As I daydream, I stare in to the unknown
Knowing that the daylight has me prone
My eyes make love to the sunlight, like it turns them on
I'm all alone with no noise, ring … ring … I refuse to answer the phone
I listen to God on the inside of me, as questions are answered and clues are shown
And he doesn't just speak to me, he hums to the animals through the wind blown
I'm not a child, but intently I listen even though I'm grown
Leaving with me- ideas that I lone
With strength and bass, but gentle is his tone
But staring into the unknown, I do condone

4 the Saints

Does a God-fearing person, speak without rehearsing
Can a spiritual person, not wear a fitted backward cap
Will a young Godly person, be ashamed to praise God with a rap
Which is worse, a spiritual person that drinks, smokes or curse
Would a Christian have money and pass someone who begs for food and thirst
Should a fellow saint be slow to commend and fast to condemn

Does a God-fearing person- not apply the Bible
Can a spiritual person- be not reliable
Will a young Godly person- fear testifying about being delivered from HIV
Hypothetically, which is worse, allowing people's judgment's to stop me- or being a footstool to the enemy
Would a Christian think to judge, based on looks and deny me
Should a fellow saint believe less in God's healing and greater is the meds

Does a God-fearing person, run from the FEDS
Can a spiritual person, speak as if they're a judge
Will a young Godly person, react quickly off of an accidental nudge
Which is worse, the views of the unsterilized, or negative tongues that aren't paralyzed
Would a Christian give raw uncut words, that come to others as a surprise
Should a fellow saint, act as if it's a sin for a guy to wear braids

Does a God-fearing person- personify the guy with a hair cut preferably with a fade
Can a spiritual person, love to stay in conflict and criticize
Will a young Godly person, work out on God's words, and think of it as being exercise
Which is worse, a spiritual person that can't keep their eyes at bay, or hating thy neighbor who is gay
Would a Christian see this type of person and avoid saying hey
Should a fellow saint believe in praising rituals

Does praise start with relations with God, that are considered consensual
Can a spiritual person, look at a brother and think that they dress holier than another
Will a young Godly person – fear, surrender, and allow God to have complete submission
Which is worse: praise being a thing of competition, or another saint speaking against your mission
Would a Christian purposely misconstrue the word
Or should a fellow saint, read for themselves and deny what they've heard

Ground Zero
(the Start)

Here I still stand
On God's words and solid land
After a devastating collapse
Now my mind is a computer running long, laps
Grounded was a building, with sixty-five floors
The aftermath left, a front and back door
Gone is the old
But only to make way for the new, to unfold
I asked God for the sketches to the new design
And he gave me something all new and redefined
But first he gave me a much-needed seven-day vacation
And planted in my mind his thoughts, concerning a brilliant
foundation
So I listened and took them to heart
And now I stand on God's words and ground zero the start

Behind closed eyes

I close my eyes and the light vanishes
Into the darkness of night; goes the appearance
But God shows beauty in the dark figment
With this large mass that has no brightness in its pigment
It's truly a wonder how I can see something
Where realistically I'm supposed to see nothing
I see activity, in mid-air
My sight is focused and I see the expanded picture
And I hear a familiar voice, humbly state "I'm still here with ya"
For the first time in my life I view perfection
Perfect choreography with no needed correction
Complete untouched beauty, is what I see
Finally envisioning the work of the architect who devised me
I see the greatest house party
And out of all the folk present- no one chose to be absent or tardy
I see mighty angels, diverse like a mixed flavor
I'm so close; I can feel the presence of my Savior

No lie

I refuse to sing the dreary blues
I'm going to tell the Good News
It's all about maintaining and following the correct rules
But still you got throwback brothas, that'll give anything for some
land and a mule
In this world filled with negative, God still sends many positive clues
So daily I read the basic instructions before leaving this earth
And if God continues to spare my life, I will teach my seed the truth
after birth
See my seed won't grow to be anybody's inferior
'Cause in this life, too many believe the wrong people to be superior
See the most priceless thing is knowledge, it's not expensive
As a matter of fact, the only thing you may have to pay, is attention
to become
comprehensive
Instead we study each other, like research that's extensive
'Cause the truth is always made clear, even at times when it's compressed
We as people have to learn how important it is to stay abreast
Furthermore, we have to learn the difference between a test, and us
creating a mess

A lesson retained

On this day I inhale new air
'Cause yesterday I felt the wear and tear
God handled the task with delicate care
And now absent is the surreal nightmare
Obviously we take for granted how situations-
can be unfair
And how fools travel in pairs
But we must not get caught up in despair
God is good, and the love is felt and shared

RIP 2 yesterday

A feel of pain
Showing no sorrow
I would love to borrow

Happiness
A low diss
I have 2 dismiss
Tomorrow I will kiss

C you at the finish line
(My 23rd race)

I'm out of the gates
Out of the box
However, this time it's strenuous, like running barefooted on rocks
So I'm truly disengaged; sprinting like a man that's in a hurry to flee
his present
But at the same time, feeling like a man that's on a treadmill
Having too much time to kill
At that moment, I run a path that was fixed
With a mind filled with emotions, that seems mixed
Feeling like I'm just doing this for my health
So I glance to my left and right, and only see periods of myself
This isn't even a real race
But instead, this may very well be, the battle of my life
I look behind me to my left, and see the allusion of a younger me;
that quickly becomes my ex with a knife
Back-stabbing, huh
Thank God I didn't slow down on my run
To my right is a more consistent me, no matter the age or the distant
This allusion, becomes my angel with wings, pushing me
Motivating me; come on, E
So methodically I push, I run, I no longer look back
But this event becomes even more packed
More roadblocks, more women, and more old and new faces
I ask my angel, is it always this congested; at all the races
He responds. "This is your home going or homecoming celebration.
You choose," and then I feel my feet gain elevation
While ascending I question, where's the finish line, he says up.
My eyes flood, with enough tears to overflow a cup
His last statement is, meet you at the finish line.

My worth

Why should I make an appointment with death to get recognized
I'm worth more alive than dead, or maybe I'm too far ahead
My birth right is to express my life, So now I exercise
My moment has long been realized
But to some, me stating my opinions and
facts, may seem as a bit of a surprise
But the next generation's stride ushers in a new rise
However the illustrious old school and I have connected ties
For some of my complex traits have grown from former allies
So to my followers and comrades, question
me and I'll graciously give my replies
Since my last appearance, my position has somewhat
changed; but the quality I've reprised
And some thoughts from yesterday, have been revised
I sit back and just visualize
And only after that, part do I analyze
For those of you who don't speak well, I
translate your sensitive cries
'Cause that's where the most humbling trait to humanity lies
Each day as the time flies, I work to reach further than the skies
This is why I don't grasp being worth more dead than
alive, so I'll hold out on my final good-byes

Trapped in the hotel

Unconcerned people ask you questions like they care
I'm sitting here wondering if there's room for the good in a neutral hotel
My conscience wants an answer, so if you know, do tell
Especially when it seems like this hotel is run by heathens
All I hear is reckless breathing
Covered issues surface like, a rooted relationship with my father
So many disappointments got me feeling like why bother
Angry with the guy now for no reason- like he just created treason
But it'll get better, is the statement, that has the pain easing
A person being them self; is the only thing out of a person- I trust
And proven action is the solution, resulting in the answer, making
the A+
'Cause in the hotel you should be about addition, and the admission
But I've seen the division and the ruthless submission
I want to show the others what I see, but I need their permission
In order for me to accomplish my mission

Ice, water, fire, and smoke

In its most sculpted form it's ice
In its most creative form it's water
In its most fierce form it's fire
In its most settled form its smoke
But at its most deadly form, it's all of the above
Ice, water, fire, and smoke
Call it ice, 'cause that's a solid reaction
And truth establishes the cold nature of this action
Call it water 'cause it flows unrehearsed, and unrestricted
And it rises to cover surfaces as this dominant liquid
Call it fire, 'cause a spark gives it the hunger to spread
It's the heat cleansing agent; it takes and it gives as it's fed
Call it smoke, 'cause it's the aftermath that forms the fume
It's the combined touch of the final two, appearing in a dark manner
of doom

Poetry

Poetry embodies the true form of sultry
In my eyes it's the epitome, which can display forms of floetry
It's knowing who you are, know where you've come from, well something like your family tree
You don't believe me, well go take the voyage for yourself, simply put go see
I'm a young man living proof, I know where I come from; I know who I be
See listen carefully to the knowledge I'm giving you, and you'll soon figure out that this is truly a freebie
Poetry can be more than defining and rhyming words, it can be opening a lock with a stellar key
It could also be stating how you feel using the means of infuses and clarity
It could be explaining your motivational struggle or telling your very own exploration
To some, poetry is medication, meditation, and even education
It's the way to cut a problem without a weapon such as a blade or knife
It's a universal language and culture, together it's a way of life

It's Poetry!

RAW
&
UNCUT

Why she got to be on the same level as your mutt
Or better yet … why she got to be called a slut
And why you got to add fire to his wood, by showing ya butt
Why you got to slap her and tell her to keep her mouth shut
Or better yet why you work for him placing yourself in a rut
Why when she ask you if you ready for the baby,
the answer comes out like a maybe
Or better yet … why when she wants some paper work from you-
You quickly answer, come on, baby
And why you got to sit there, do nothing and collect, like thank
God this baby saved me
Why she got to hold the fort down
Or better yet … why she and the child have to suffer and frown
And why you got to take you frustration out on the child,
By beating the infant down
Why you feel like she's got to be like you, so you stone her
Or better yet … why she gets no say so, is it because you feel
like you own her
And why you got to poison that child by telling them-
they have no father, he was a sperm donor
Why you got to rip off her bra
Or better yet … why you didn't stop when the child saw
And why you didn't leave the first time you got hit in your jaw

Later ... to be cont'd

Thanks for your company, but now I must minimize the power
For now has come the designated rest hour
A lot of people take this time to say, the end
But when the time is right I'll just press play, and once again begin
So no, I'm not finished
'Cause with things still happening in the world, my lyrics makeup
to cover the blemish
I won't even give goodbyes because I'll be telling you hi, like it's
tomorrow; you know time flies
So I'm gone until next time, even if that's a surprise in the form of
the next sunrise
And hopefully I'll age like wine, and come back more knowledgably
sophisticated and better
Like a refreshing breeze with the changing of the weather
So remember, we don't say goodbye no more; we just cater the term later
Hope you enjoyed the diverse topics on this menu
And the changing of the venue
I really don't want to wear out my next welcome before I begin ... so
I'll leave you with a – to be continued.

Edwards Brothers Malloy
Thorofare, NJ USA
May 18, 2016